More Trouble at Trebizon

5p

This is the fifth title in the Trebizon series. You can read more about Rebecca Mason and her friends in:

Also by Anne Digby in Granada Children's Books:

Anne Digby

More Trouble at Trebizon

Illustrated by Gavin Rowe

A DRAGON BOOK

GRANADA

London Toronto Sydney New York

Published by Granada Publishing Limited in 1982

ISBN 0 583 30434 6

Copyright © Anne Digby 1981

Granada Publishing Limited
Frogmore, St Albans, Herts AL2 2NF
and
36 Golden Square, London W1R 4AH
866 United Nations Plaza, New York, NY 10017, USA
117 York Street, Sydney, NSW 2000, Australia
100 Skyway Avenue, Rexdale, Ontario, M9W 3A6, Canada
61 Beach Road, Auckland, New Zealand

Printed and bound in Great Britain by
Cox & Wyman Ltd, Reading

Granada ®
Granada Publishing ®

To Alan

Contents

1
The Very Important Person

Rebecca Mason's taxi turned in through the wrought iron gates. Back to school! This was going to be her fifth term at Trebizon.

A big black car was right on their tail, but Rebecca didn't even notice it. As the taxicab crawled along the narrow, wooded drive, observing the 10 m.p.h. speed limit, she fidgeted in the back seat and looked ahead, not behind. She was impatient to see her five friends again.

'I'll be last back!' she thought. 'I always am when I stay at Gran's. What's new? What's everyone been up to in the Christmas holidays?'

She already knew some of the news.

Elf had been ski-ing. Rebecca had received a postcard from Switzerland.

Tish and Sue and Margot, who all lived in or around London, had been to a big pop concert with three of the Garth College boys – Mike Brown, Chris Earl-Smith and Curly Watson. They had been friendly with Mike since surfing last summer, and apparently had met the other two at that end-of-term Christmas party at the boys' boarding house. Garth College was only three miles from Trebizon and both Tish and Sue had elder brothers there. *Chris and Curly are the same age as us, like Mike,* Tish had written to Rebecca. *It turns out they all live in London. When the three of them are together they really make you laugh.*

It might have made Rebecca feel rather dull, spending the Christmas holidays at her grandmother's bungalow in Gloucestershire. But the weather had been mild and she had been able to play tennis nearly every day with some good local players there. She had found it all quite exciting.

Of the six friends, only Mara had been up to nothing whatsoever.

10

Father is being so strict. I feel like a prisoner, Mara had written from Athens. *The Grigoris affair has upset him and I have never known him so bad. He lets me have no freedom at all. He was even angry that Curly Watson wrote me a letter! I cannot wait to get back to school. I simply cannot wait.*

Mara's father, a Greek shipowner, was one of the world's richest men. Rebecca had no idea what the Grigoris affair was, but she knew that Mr Leonodis tended to keep his daughter wrapped in a protective cocoon. It was funny to think that an English boarding school, for Mara, represented freedom! Rebecca's own first impressions of Trebizon had been just the reverse.

'But it's great being in Court House,' Rebecca admitted. 'All those rules and regulations we had in Juniper...No cycling...No going downtown... Wouldn't want to go back to all that. Wouldn't ever want to be a junior again!'

Or so Rebecca thought from the dizzy heights of being a member of the middle school. In actual fact they'd all enjoyed their spell in Juniper, the big boarding house for juniors. But Court House was different again and the six friends revelled in the free-and-easy atmosphere of a small boarding house of only thirty six girls, set well away from the main school buildings.

The woods petered out into open parkland and in the distance the fine old manor house that formed the heart of the school came in sight. Rebecca wound down the window of the taxi and stuck her head out, pleased by the view. Ancient oak trees, gnarled and mossy-boled, stood firm and solid in the undulating parkland. They

11

were serene and unbowed in the landscape, their bare branches black against the sky. Rebecca could just make out some wild deer grazing, their brown coats flickering among tussocks of faded winter grass. The January sky was leaden grey, as if snow were about to fall.

The drive curved round and the school came into full view, face on. A momentary parting of the clouds let through a rod of sunlight that illuminated the front of the old building. The facade of the former manor house, as though picked out by a spotlight, became almost luminous against the deep, dark backdrop of heavy skies. Rebecca stared, thinking of it long ago, with carriages and horses at the door.

The car behind hooted.

'We'll let him go by, shall we?' said the taxi-driver, pulling over. It was a big black saloon car, bulbous and heavy, old-fashioned looking. It had a foreign number plate and a left-hand drive.

The driver was a massive-shouldered man in a purple jumper. He was completely bald. As the car overtook them, Rebecca quickly drew her head in. The driver gave a thick-lipped smile and a genial wave.

'There are blinds at the back windows!' said Rebecca in surprise. 'Who on earth can be inside?'

'Some V.I.P. That's a bullet-proof car if you ask me!' commented the taxi-driver.

Rebecca watched the car as it swept on towards old building. It seemed to be making for the main entrance. She would like to have seen the car stop, to find out who the passenger was behind those mysterious blinds. But there was no chance. The turn-off to Court House was just ahead.

'We fork right here!' said Rebecca quickly. 'Down this track. It's a short cut to my boarding house.'

They turned into the narrow track, past the rhododendron bushes.

'Playing tennis this term then?' the driver asked. He had noticed two rackets strapped to Rebecca's trunk. 'I thought you young ladies played hockey in the winter.'

'I'll be doing winter tennis training,' said Rebecca. She hesitated. 'At Exonford. I'm a county junior.' As he gave a whistle she added quickly: 'Only in the D squad. So far.'

'You born in this shire, then?' He was surprised. 'You sound London to me.'

'I am London, really. But I was born in the west country. Dad was working down here the year I was born. That's why I can play for the county here – if ever I get good enough, that is.'

'Hard work, eh?'

'Very.'

They had passed the Hilary Camberwell Music School and the lake. Now Court House came in view. It was such a pleasant, mellow old house, with all its little rooms, thought Rebecca. The creeper was bare at this time of year, but the building still looked pretty. The sight of it made her feel happy.

'Rebeck's here!' cried Tish Anderson joyfully as the taxi crunched to a halt. She'd been watching out for her.

She was first out of the front door, followed closely by Sue Murdoch and Margot Lawrence. They thronged round Rebecca as she got out of the taxi and Sue threw an arm around her neck.

'We've been waiting for you!'

'Elf's watching the fudge! A second batch!' said Margot. 'The first batch is cool and she's putting it out.'

'Putting it away, more like it!' said Rebecca. They all loved Sally Elphinstone but she had a bigger-than-average appetite and a figure to match.

'Even Elf couldn't put all this away,' said Tish. 'We can't wait to get started!'

'And I'm last as usual.' Rebecca said, wryly. 'Sorry, it's the coach journey.'

'No, you're not last,' said Margot. 'Mara's not here yet.'

'Isn't she?' Rebecca got her purse out to pay the taxi-driver. He had taken her luggage into Court House and put it in the hall for her. Now he was coming back. 'What's happened to Mara?'

'I expect the mini's got stuck in some traffic jam,' said Tish.

Mara's elder brother, Anestis, usually brought her to school in his little red car, as she wasn't allowed to travel any distance on her own. The Greek boy was at university in England.

Rebecca paid the taxi driver and gave him a tip.

'Good luck with the tennis, miss,' he said, just before he drove off.

'Thanks!'

The others pushed Rebecca in through the front door of Court House. Her trunk was waiting for her in the hall, just by the common room door. They chattered excitedly.

'You should have seen my report,' said Tish. 'Mrs Leonard was horrible to me!'

'Well, you were horrible to *her* – ' said Rebecca.

'Never mind Mrs Leonard,' said Sue. 'Tell her about Fenners tonight – '

'Fenners?' asked Rebecca. Fenners was a big coffee place at the top end of Trebizon High Street. 'What about it?'

'We're meeting the boys there at six o'clock!' said Margot. The black girl grinned. 'We fixed it up on the train down.'

'They're dying to meet you, Rebeck,' said Tish.

'And Curly wants to see Mara again,' said Sue breathlessly.

'They've got some plans for this term,' Tish butted in, 'and they want to include us in.'

'Sounds fun,' agreed Rebecca. They were standing outside the common room now, just near her trunk. 'Help me round to the room with my luggage, will you – '

She suddenly stopped. The common room door was wide open and she could see inside. She nudged Tish and pointed.

'Who's she?' she whispered.

Some Fourth Years were lolling in the chintzy armchairs in the common room, watching television, but Rebecca was looking past them, to the far corner of the room. A tiny girl with long brown plaits was sitting bolt upright in a chair, reading a book. Her Trebizon uniform, which was too big for her, looked brand new.

'New girl,' replied Tish.

'But what's she doing making herself at home in *our* common room?' whispered Rebecca indignantly. 'She should be over in Juniper House with the other juniors.'

'No she shouldn't – ' began Tish.

'Come on Rebecca!' said Sue. The other two were already starting to drag her trunk along the hall, towards her room, which lay along a side corridor. 'It's rude to stare.'

'She's going in the room opposite ours,' Tish continued. She was laughing. 'It looks like a mistake, but it isn't. She's going in with the two Annes – Aba's not coming back till next term. They've got Lucy in Aba's place. She's going to be in III Alpha with us, as well.'

'In our form?' asked Rebecca. 'But she looks so young – '

'She is! But, you see, she's a genius. Her mother's just been telling us. Come on, Rebeck, Elf's waiting – '

'Her mother?' mouthed Rebecca in fascination, still hanging back. 'What's her mother doing at Trebizon?'

'Living in staff quarters. A new teacher. Going to teach us geography. Mrs Hubbard.'

'Old Mother Hubbard!' squeaked Rebecca.

'Sssh!' giggled Tish, clamping a hand over Rebecca's mouth.

Lucy Hubbard suddenly stood up, book in hand.

'She's heard!' thought Rebecca.

But no such thing. The new girl was glaring, not at Rebecca, but at the television set. It was on fairly loud.

'D'you mind?' she said, in a prim rather grown-up voice. 'Some of us are trying to read.'

The Fourth Years laughed.

'Of course we don't mind.'

16

'Read as much as you like – '

'But – ' Lucy's voice faltered. Were they deliberately not getting the point? Margaret Exton gave the answer.

'Shut up and sit down, pipsqueak.'

Tish dragged Rebecca away.

'Do you think she's going to fit in?' said Rebecca.

'Who knows,' shrugged Tish. 'Her mother's much worse than she is.'

The two of them shared a room with Sue and they got there just in time to help hump Rebecca's trunk to the foot of her bed.

While Rebecca was unpacking, Elf appeared from the kitchen.

'Rebecca!' she cheered. Then she looked at her watch solemnly. 'Do you realise Mara still isn't here? If we don't start the fudge soon it'll spoil our tea!'

Everyone agreed that that would be a serious matter.

'Let's start!'

'We don't have to eat it all.'

'The second lot's still hot, so we can't!'

'There'll be plenty left for Mara!'

Rebecca left her trunk half unpacked and trooped into the kitchen with the others. As she stared at Elf's delicious creamy brown fudge her mouth watered. Sue made a pot of tea and they all ate and talked and laughed a lot.

'Really, that's your third piece of fudge, Rebecca. Whatever next?'

'My fourth, I guess!'

It was fun to be back! But why was Mara so late?

'I won't cut the second batch yet,' said Elf. 'Not without Mara.'

'Let's save it for tonight,' suggested Margot. They were all starting to feel rather full. 'After we get back from Fenners.'

'I shall start my diet again tomorrow,' vowed Elf.

'Did you know?' said Rebecca, who loved storing up useless facts, 'that you use up more calories in the act of eating a stick of celery than the celery itself contains?'

'Don't believe it!' scoffed Tish.

'Then if I lived on celery, I'd get thinner and thinner – ' said Elf.

'Better than that!' laughed Rebecca. 'You'd completely disappear. – Help!' She ducked as Elf hurled a packet of tea at her. It sailed straight past her head and out through the open window. 'Now look what you've done!'

Margot nipped out of the kitchen door and into the courtyard at the back to retrieve the packet of tea. It didn't even belong to them! As she picked it up, she caught sight of a familiar figure at the Barringtons' back door. He was talking to Mrs Barrington, their house mistress.

'Guess what!' she said, bursting back into the kitchen. 'Anestis – I've just seen Anestis! He's out there talking to Mrs Barry. So where's Mara?'

'Yippee!' said Tish, leading the rush into the front hall. 'She must have arrived. Let's see if the car's outside – '

'There's a car – ' Sue whispered, opening the front door. 'But it's not the sort Anestis usually drives – '

'It's like a gangster's car!' cried Tish. 'The sort you see in old films on T.V!'

'It's the V.I.P. car!' exclaimed Rebecca in amazement. 'It was just behind my taxi.'

The big black saloon was parked in front of the boarding house. Its driver, the bald man in the purple sweater, was standing beside it, arms folded. He was very big, built like a wrestler, Rebecca thought. She could just imagine him grunting. But he had quite a friendly face. The girls hung back by the front door, taking stock of the situation.

'Where's Mara?' said Tish.

'She must be sitting in the back of the car,' said Sue, in awe. 'Behind those blinds. What's going on?'

'Maybe she's got chicken pox,' giggled Elf, nervously.

'Who's the man?' whispered Margot. 'He's huge.'

'Well, let's go and ask him!' suggested Rebecca. She was intrigued. To think Mara had been in that car all along! Why had they gone over to main school, first?

Even as she stepped out on to the gravelled forecourt, Anestis appeared from around the corner of the Barringtons' quarters, with Mrs Barrington. The house mistress strode over to the parked car and opened the back passenger door.

'Come on, Mara,' she said sharply. 'You can't sit there sulking all afternoon. Come and see your friends, and get unpacked – '

The big man lifted some cases out of the boot while Anestis held it open for him. Mrs Barrington pulled Mara out of the car.

Rebecca and the others could see at once that Mara

19

was in a bad mood, tearful and rebellious.

'I don't want him hanging round, I don't!' she exclaimed, pointing at the hulking figure. He stood there, a suitcase in each hand, smiling and immoveable. 'Tell him he must go back to Athens now!'

'Impossible.' Mrs Barrington took Mara by the arm and steered her across the gravel towards Rebecca & Co. 'Your father has given strict instructions. Now, go and have a wash and tidy up after your journey and you'll feel better.'

She deposited Mara with them and hurried off. They all surrounded their friend, hugged her, and bore her into Court House.

'Cheer up!'

'What's going on?'

Somehow Mara managed to summon up a weak version of her usual lovely warm smile. 'Oh! It's good to see you!'

'What about that man?' asked Rebecca. 'Who *is* he?'

'His name is Papa.' Mara was obviously very embarrassed. Angry tears brimmed up again in her brown eyes. 'It is stupid. It is humiliating!'

'He's your father – ?' began Elf, in surprise.

Mara shook her head vehemently, just as the big man came into the hall.

'Mara, show Papa where to put your luggage – ' said Anestis.

Mara deliberately turned her back on them. 'You know where our room is. Show him yourself!' Then she ran the full length of the hall and disappeared into the kitchen, slamming the door loudly behind her. Girls were hanging over the banisters, to see what was going on. Lucy Hubbard had put her book down and ventured to the door of the common room, full of curiosity.

'This way,' Margot said to the big man. 'We'll show you.'

They turned up the little corridor off the main hall, all in a troupe, and jostled into the pretty room, next door to Rebecca's, that Mara shared with Margot and Elf. The man deposited the suitcases by the bed.

'I'll introduce you to Mara's friends,' said Anestis. 'Then we can go.' He repeated the words in Greek. Then: 'Girls, this is Mr Papaconstantopoulos, Papa for short.'

They all shook hands in turn.

'Papa used to be a wrestler,' said Anestis. Rebecca had been right about that, then. 'But you will find that he is a very kind, gentle person. He is retained by my father. He is a long-standing and faithful friend of the Leonodis family. He has helped my father many times,' he added, as though that explained everything perfectly.

The big Greek beamed and nodded.

Rebecca and Tish and Sue exchanged baffled glances. Elf coughed.

They all came out of the room in a bunch and there was noise and scampering in the corridor as some girls scattered. 'Eavesdroppers!' said Margot scornfully. The friends then hung back as Anestis went along to the door of the kitchen and knocked.

'Mara!' he bent his face close to the door. 'I'm taking Papa down to his hotel now and will see that everything

21

is comfortable for him. We shall have a meal and this evening I shall catch my train.'

Silence.

Anestis shrugged philosophically and turned away from the door.

'She's taking it hard,' he said to the girls. 'But father has made up his mind and that is that. Try and get her used to the idea.'

The dark, good-looking Greek boy went off with his hulking companion. The friends were mystified but Tish was the first to recover. She raced after Anestis and caught him at the front door, while Papaconstantopoulos ambled on ahead, making for the parked car.

'Get used to *what* idea?'

'Having Papa around. He is going to be living at the Trebizon Bay Hotel. Father thinks it is necessary.'

'*Living* there? What – all term? D'you mean he's – sort of – going to be – Mara's bodyguard?'

'Correct!'

As Anestis left, Tish hurried back to the others.

'Did you hear that?' she exclaimed.

'Of course we heard!' said Rebecca.

The idea took some getting used to. Mara was the V.I.P. – the Very Important Person! She'd come back to school complete with her own personal bodyguard and a bullet-proof car!

Why?

Poor Mara, thought Rebecca.

The five friends surged towards the kitchen to find her.

2
Meeting the Boys

'It might be fun,' said Tish. 'I mean, we could get him to take us places in that great gangster car – '

'Fun?' said Mara, outraged. 'Having a watchdog!

Having someone spying on you! Don't say that, Tish, even in joke.'

'We're only trying to cheer you up,' said Sue, feebly.

'Have some fudge,' begged Elf. 'Look, this is still the first batch.'

Mara's expression softened. She was hungry after her journey. 'Thanks, Elf. Mmmmm.' The fudge was delicious! 'How many pieces can I have?' She cocked an ear. 'Was that the car? Have they gone?'

Rebecca was nearest. She opened the kitchen door and squinted out, right down the hall, to the front door. She saw a flash of black go past.

'Gone!' she confirmed.

'Good!' Mara sighed, relaxed and sank her teeth into the next piece of fudge. 'Anything to drink? Oh, it's good to be back, I guess. I have had the most terrible holidays! And this is the last straw, this Papa nonsense!'

'Can't you more or less ignore him?' suggested Elf. 'Pretend he's not there when you go down town and he follows you around – '

'If only I could!' said Mara. 'But you see – '

She stopped.

'See what?' asked Rebecca, curious to know what Mara had been about to say.

'Oh, nothing.'

'Tea or coffee?' asked Sue.

'Er – coffee please,' said Mara. She looked thoughtful for a moment and then her annoyance bubbled up again. 'The whole thing is mad! This crazy idea my father has got. That I go down town and somebody kidnaps me or something!'

'What's got into him then?' asked Tish. 'He's never worried about your being here before. I mean, Trebizon's such a safe, peaceful sort of place – '

'Exactly! Exactly!' Mara nodded her head in violent agreement. 'You think I haven't told him that! A hundred times! But, he has got this stupid bee buzzing in his bonnet and...' She shrugged her shoulders, helplessly. 'Oh, let's talk about something else.'

'Let's!' said Margot and Elf in unison, more than anxious to see their room-mate simmer down and become her usual sunny self. 'Er – '

'Have you seen Elf's second batch of fudge?' asked Margot, saying the first thing that came into her head. 'Show her. Elf!'

'Fantastic!' exclaimed Mara, as Elf brought it over. 'Only – I can't manage any more just yet.'

'None of us can,' said Sue, placing a cup of coffee on the table in front of her. 'We'll save it till we get back. Cycling always makes you starving hungry.'

'Get back, from where?' asked Mara. 'What cycling?'

'Fenners!' exclaimed Margot.

'Fenners?'

'We're going there after tea.' Tish informed her. She raised her famous grin and twirled around, her short dark curls bouncing. 'We fixed it up with the boys on the train. Don't look so worried. What's the matter, aren't your lights working?'

'Am I invited?' asked Mara in a still little voice.

'Are *you* invited?' exclaimed Tish. 'Mara – what a daft question! You know how much they all like you – '

'Especially Curly Watson!' giggled Sue. 'Oh, Mara.

We're *all* invited. The boys have got something going on this term and they need our help.'

Mara frowned over her coffee cup, as though the act of drinking it required intense concentration. She drained it down and banged it on to the table, then jumped up and flung her arms wide. She looked, quite suddenly elated.

'I've decided. I'm coming!'

'You bet you're coming!' said Tish. 'Come on, let's get cleared up in here before Mrs Barry finds all the mess. Elf, what are we going to do about that fudgy saucepan? It's all stuck up round the side.'

'I'll clean it,' said Margot. 'Come on, where's the pot scourer – ?'

'Mara,' said Sue, 'you and Rebecca had better get unpacked!'

Everybody was happy because Mara was happy again.

It was only afterwards, as she finished her unpacking, that it occurred to Rebecca that Mara's hesitation had been slightly odd. What did she mean about deciding? What was there to decide about?

The first tea bell went in all the boarding houses and the exodus began. In no time at all, Court House was empty and silent. So was Norris, over the back. Further away, girls poured from Sterndale, Tavistock and Chambers. The dark grounds became alive with them all as they processed along well-lit footpaths towards the main school buildings, which were set round a quadrangle.

The former manor house itself contained class rooms, the main library and school offices. It was known as old school and the quadrangle gardens lay at the back of it.

The gardens were enclosed on one side by a modern white block that housed the dining hall, on the ground floor, the assembly hall above and the art room, science laboratories and home economics rooms above that. Juniper House, the long red brick building where more than a hundred juniors lived, formed another side of the quadrangle. Staff living quarters, once a block for horses, carriages and grooms, with clock tower high above, completed the square.

The quadrangle gardens, protectively enclosed and suffused with shadowy light from the buildings on all sides, echoed with voices and laughter as girls streamed along the terrace and into the dining hall for tea.

'Made it!' laughed Rebecca as she and Tish scuttled in through the doors, just as the second bell went. They'd been loitering along the lakeside path, deep in conversation about the holidays, and had nearly made themselves late. 'Look, Sue and Mara are waving.'

They threaded their way through the crowded dining hall and got to the table where Sue had saved them two places. They were just about to sit down when a member of staff bore down on Tish, towing a small girl along behind her.

'One moment, Ishbel.'

'What's Tish done now?' wondered Rebecca. They'd only just got back to school! The teacher looked new – a dumpy woman with red hair.

'Yes, Mrs Hubbard?' replied Tish.

Of course! Mother Hubbard and daughter, realised Rebecca.

'Lucy can't seem to find a place,' said the new geography mistress.

'There's an empty place over there,' said Tish, pointing to one of the Second Year tables. 'Between Eleanor Keating and Susannah Skelhorn. They're very nice, both of them.' She looked at Lucy and grinned. 'I mean, they won't bite or anything.'

'If you're a new junior you'll find they're good fun to know,' Mara joined in. She was relaxed and friendly and seemed to have put all thought of Papa out of her mind. 'Eleanor's in the Under-14 hockey team and Susannah – she's editor of the Juniper Journal. We used to call it the J.J. As a matter of fact, we started it – '

Mrs Hubbard cut her off in mid-sentence.

'Juniors? Lucy isn't going into the juniors. She's very

28

advanced for her age. Ishbel knows all about it.' She gave Tish a confiding smile. 'Suffice to say that Miss *Welbeck* herself agrees that Lucy is a very special case. She's going to live in Court House and take her lessons with form III Alpha. I'm sure it'll be a great success!'

Miss Welbeck was the principal of Trebizon School.

'Oh,' said Mara. The others already knew this not-very-exciting piece of news. But Mara had been much too het up earlier to notice or care that there was someone new in Court House. Now she stared at the diminutive figure with the plaits and the too-big uniform in some astonishment. 'That's our form,' she added, lamely.

'Good, good!' said Mrs Hubbard briskly. She stared pointedly at the two empty seats. Tish and Rebecca were still hovering by them, wondering whether they should sit down or not. 'Lucy can start to – to – '

'Integrate,' said Lucy firmly. She pulled one of the chairs out.

'Grate, you mean,' muttered Sue. She'd had one conversation with the new girl over at the boarding house and found that enough.

'What did you say? The girl in glasses?' asked Mrs Hubbard sharply.

'She said the chair seems to grate!' somebody chipped in quickly.

'Er – squeaks a bit, too,' added Tish. 'When you pull it out – ' Everybody started snorting and trying not to giggle. A red flush crept slowly up Mrs Hubbard's neck. But Tish looked the picture of innocence. 'Toss you for the other chair, Rebecca.'

'No, no, it's fine!' Rebecca gasped, fighting off a strong desire to laugh. She turned away quickly. She could see an empty place next to Josselyn Vining over on another table. She wanted to talk to Joss, anyway, about county tennis coaching! 'See you afterwards.'

The only person not to be amused was Mara. What was this miniature doing in Court House? You were supposed to be at least thirteen! Even worse, her mother appeared to have joined the school staff. A teacher's daughter living in Court House with them! Mara's heart sank a little.

As if she hadn't got enough problems!

The six friends cycled off through the school grounds as fast as they could go, their lights bobbing along the dark drive.

'What d'you want to go down town in the dark for?' the duty prefect had asked them, outside the dining hall. 'All the shops will be shut.'

'We're only going to Fenners to have a coffee!'

'Meeting some of the Garth boys there, I expect.'

Fortunately at that moment Pippa Fellowes-Walker had sauntered up to see what was going on. She was Rebecca's favourite prefect.

'And why not? Oh, let 'em go, Edwina. This is about the only week night in the whole term when nobody's got any prep.'

'All right then. Check your lights. Wear your capes, it's cold. Behave yourselves and be back by half-past seven.'

'*Thanks!*'

30

They hurried off and Lucy Hubbard had stood on the terrace, watching them go, her eyes wide with interest.

Soon the friends were cycling out of the main gates and along the top road, which was unlit. Across the fields was the dark mass of Trebizon Bay. Turning her head to look out to sea, Rebecca could see the lights of a big tanker. The town lay just ahead of them, glowing orange in the night sky. She glanced at Mara, cycling alongside her, black hair streaming out, eyes watering a little, cape billowing.

She was pedalling fast, for Mara.

'I feel so free!' said the Greek girl, suddenly. 'Like a bird flying out of a cage!'

A few large snowflakes began to fall and they all laughed.

'We just escaped in time!'

'They'd never have let us go if they'd known it was going to snow!'

It was sheer delight to park their bikes and walk in out of the cold, into the warm, noisy coffee shop, ten minutes' later. Snowflakes were still clinging to their capes. Three boys rose up from a table and came over to meet them. Rebecca spotted Mike Brown at once. They'd known him quite a long time, through Sue's brothers, David and Edward. The one with straight dark hair was presumably Chris Earl-Smith because obviously the short fair-haired one, with curly hair, was Curly Watson.

He made a bee-line for Mara.

'Mara!'

'Curly!'

He took her hand in his and she let him and it seemed very natural somehow. Rebecca thought they looked right together.

At the same time, Rebecca glanced uneasily around the coffee place. She half-expected to see the bulky figure of Papa sitting silently in a corner somewhere, keeping watch over Mara.

But of course, he was nowhere to be seen.

'He's only just getting settled into his hotel this evening!' Rebecca reminded herself. 'I bet that's why

Mara feels so happy and carefree! He'll probably start his duties in earnest tomorrow. I wonder what being a bodyguard entails?'

'No need to look,' said Tish, out of the corner of her mouth. She'd read Rebecca's mind. 'He's not here.'

'Stop plotting you two,' said Mike, taking each of them by an arm and steering them towards the table. 'We'll pull some extra chairs over so we can all squash round. Rebecca, you haven't met Chris yet –'

'Hallo,' said Chris.

'And this is Curly –'

Curly and Mara were already sitting down and deep in conversation. He gave Rebecca a quick grin and then carried on.

'I guessed,' said Rebecca, smiling.

They all crammed round the table together and were soon chatting and laughing and drinking coffee. The boys had a never-ending stream of funny stories to tell – and Tish had a few of her own.

'Whatever it is we're meeting them about, it's obviously nothing urgent,' thought Rebecca. She didn't mind! The coffee was thick and creamy and she felt warm again. They'd get round to it in their own good time. Meanwhile, she hadn't laughed so much for ages.

Back at Court House, the telephone was ringing.

Lucy Hubbard was sitting in the common room reading a book, all alone. Because there was no prep to do, almost nobody had come back to the boarding house after tea. A lot of them had gone to the sports centre and (thought Lucy) that girl called Tish and her friends had even cycled down to the town to meet some boys...

Lucy didn't mind. She'd been half hoping that if she sat here the telephone would ring...

She rushed to answer it. 'Hallo!'

'Hallo?' It was a stanger's voice at the other end of the line and Lucy felt a dull ache of disappointment. 'Is Mara Leonodis there? This is her brother.'

'No. She's gone to a coffee bar.'

'*What?*' He sounded angry. 'Are you sure?'

A sudden glow of self-righteousness swept through Lucy.

'Of course I'm sure,' she said in her piping little voice. 'I thought she wasn't meant to!' She paused and then her wish to air her knowledge got the better of her. 'Excuse me asking, but isn't Linda Grigoris her cousin?'

3
A Greek Drama

'When are you going to shut up, Mike Brown?' said Sue,
at last.

'Eh?'

'I mean shut up impersonating Doctor Simpson and – '
Sue was smiling.

'Tell us what you're up to,' finished Tish.

'Oh, that. Yes, very important. Come on, Curly.'

Curly Watson removed his arm from round Mara's shoulders and produced a stack of printed tickets from his pockets. He started dealing them round the table to the girls, like playing cards. 'We want you to take a dozen each,' he explained. 'To sell at school.'

Mara seized one as it fell in front of her.

'A disco!' she exclaimed. 'In the school Army Cadet Hut!'

'The Electric Shock Band?' asked Margot, raising her eyebrows. 'Who are they?'

'Us!' announced Chris. 'And a few others, of course,' he added, modestly.

Sue knew that Chris was a very good trumpet player and that Curly was supposed to be quite good on drums. But –

'Not you, surely, Mike. You're tone deaf.'

'I'll be on the door, I expect. Chucker out.'

They laughed excitedly and talked about the disco. Then Rebecca noticed the date.

'Oh, Saturday week. I don't think I can come.'

She would be going to her first county tennis session at Exonford that Saturday afternoon. And there was going to be tea and a film of last year's Wimbledon championships afterwards. Joss Vining had been telling her about it.

'Oh, what a shame!'

'Poor Rebecca!' exclaimed Mara. 'Is it your tennis day?'

36

'I don't mind,' said Rebecca, truthfully. 'But don't worry, I'll help sell some tickets – I should think a lot of girls will want to go.'

'It's for Third and Fourth Years mainly,' Chris pointed out. 'Our Fifths are working hard for their mocks at the moment. They wouldn't want to come, anyway.'

'Same with ours,' said Elf.

So Robbie won't be there, thought Rebecca, thinking of Tish's brother.

'What does it mean at the bottom of the ticket, in aid of the ICF Concert expenses?' asked Elf. 'What's the ICF Concert?'

'A very big affair!' announced Curly. 'It's going to be in our school theatre, at half-term. Famous performers of all different nationalities are coming, and they're giving their services free. To raise money for the International Children's Fund – ICF.'

'Curly, needless to say, is on the committee,' commented Mike.

'Curly!' Mara gazed at him in disbelief. 'Are you really?'

'Yep.' He grinned, banged his chest and looked quite proud of himself. He was, in fact, the youngest person on the Concert Committee, which consisted mainly of senior boys, masters and their wives.

'He's even got a title,' Chris said, solemnly. 'Assistant Publicity Officer.'

'Curly!' exclaimed Mara again, more impressed than ever.

What Curly Watson lacked in height he made up for in

drive and energy. As he explained his ideas for publicizing the big concert, Rebecca began to realise that he was quite a livewire. He was hoping to raise enough money from the disco to build a travelling box office for the ICF concert!

'A travelling box office?' exclaimed Tish.

'The plan is to hire an open lorry well before the concert and turn it into a decorated float and ticket office,' explained Curly. 'It's got to be really colourful and eye-catching, of course, and we'll need some of you beautiful girls on the back in various national costumes...that's to fit in with the international theme of the concert. We'll have a three-piece band as well. Then we'll tour the town and all the surrounding villages selling tickets as we go and make sure the show's an absolute sell-out.'

'Seriously?' asked Rebecca. 'I like the sound of that!'

The boys nodded.

'The committee say okay if Curly can raise enough money to cover expenses,' Mike pointed out. 'So you'd better take those disco tickets back to school and sell the lot!'

'It's marvellous!' exclaimed Mara. She'd put her tickets in the pocket of her cape and now she clapped her hands with pleasure. Her face was shining. 'I shall sell mine and try and come back for more, Curly. A mobile box office! Can I travel on the float in a national costume – can I – can I?'

'He wants you to be the star attraction!' said Mike.

'That's right, make the rest of us jealous!' laughed Elf.

'Oh, it's *all* marvellous,' continued Mara breathlessly.

'So the disco is only the beginning! This term is going to be such fun, I know it is...'

She stopped dead. She was staring at the door. Rebecca was sitting with her back to the door, opposite her. For a moment she wondered if Mara had seen a ghost.

'What's wrong, Mara – ?' began Tish, at the same time twisting round to look. 'Oh, no – '

Her voice dropped to a whisper. Glancing back over her shoulder, Rebecca saw the huge figure of Papaconstantopoulos standing in the open doorway. He was beckoning to Mara, his bald head gleaming. The car was parked outside.

' – it's the incredible hulk,' finished Tish.

'Don't look round!' hissed Mara. 'Pretend he isn't here! Just ignore him!' She gave Curly a hard nudge. He was staring at Papa, open-mouthed. 'Stop staring. Tell a funny story or something – '

'Well, it was like this,' began Curly. 'Once upon a time – '

Elf started to giggle, from sheer nervousness. Papa was walking straight towards their table with slow, heavy steps.

He reached the table and stood towering above them all. His arms were folded and he fixed his large, friendly eyes on Mara.

'...a Scotsman, and an Irishman...'

Curly's voice trailed away to nothing. It was really rather difficult to ignore somebody so large.

'Mara?' said Papa. 'Come, please.'

'No!' hissed Mara. She shook her head furiously,

rebellious tears in her eyes. 'Go away, Papa! *Please go away*!'

The friends all held their breath. People at other tables were beginning to stare. What happens now? wondered Rebecca.

She soon had the answer.

'Excuse, please,' said Papa.

He bent forward across the table and lifted Mara clean out of her chair as though she weighed no more than a naughty three year old –

'Put me down!' shouted Mara furiously, kicking her legs.

Papa strode through Fenners, carrying Mara like a babe in arms – straight out of the door and into the night. Some boys in the corner cheered and clapped. Rebecca caught a glimpse of Anestis opening the back door of the car as Papa placed the kicking Mara inside. Then – the roar of the car engine – and they were gone.

'Well – ' gasped Curly, at last recovering his powers of speech.

'What was all that about?' asked Mike.

Tish was the first to jump to her feet. Rapidly – gazing out to where the car had been – she explained who Papa was.

'Only, it seems to be worse than we thought,' she added.

'Much worse,' agreed Rebecca. 'Poor Mara! We'd better get back as fast as we can!'

The boys scraped chairs back and let the girls out and Rebecca led the rush to the door.

'Tell Mara I'll ring her,' called Curly.

'We will.'

'And don't worry about the tickets!' Sue said, over her shoulder. 'We'll sell them okay!'

Outside, Mara's bicycle had gone. Anestis had stowed it in the big boot of the car. Rebecca dried her saddle with a corner of her school cape and then mounted. Trebizon High Street – winding downhill towards the railway station – looked rather like a Christmas card. The mellow stone buildings glowed here and there in the street lights and there was a thin covering of snow on the pavements. She turned her cycle round, pointing it out-of-town.

It had stopped snowing now.

The five friends pedalled back to Court House, as fast as they could go.

Papa drove the car up to the Barringtons' front door, round at the side of Court House. The house mistress and her husband, who was Trebizon's Director of Music, lived in a private wing attached to the main boarding house. Papa left the engine running.

'I shall be angry with you if I miss my train because of this!' Anestis said to his sister, hauling Mara out of the car. 'It was lucky I 'phoned!'

'I wish you hadn't bothered!' said Mara tearfully. 'I hate you!'

'Oh, Mara, can't you guess why I 'phoned? I wanted to talk to you! There isn't time now. Please try and see, I don't like this any more than you do. But father is father and you must obey him. Promise me – '

The front door opened and Anestis deposited Mara

with Mrs Barrington. They exchanged a few brief sentences and then Anestis ran back to the car. He had less than fifteen minutes in which to catch his train.

'My bicycle!' screamed Mara, as the car shot away. She could see it sticking out of the boot. 'I need it!'

But the car had gone.

'Please calm down, Mara,' said the house mistress in a sensible voice. 'You know perfectly well that you won't need your bicycle this term. You know exactly what your father's instructions are.'

She led Mara along the hall and then straight through a communicating door into the main part of Court House.

Alison Hissup, a Fifth Year, was just coming down the pine staircase.

'Alison!' she called. 'Mara is tired and overwrought. I want you to see that she has some cocoa, a warm shower and an early night.'

'Yes, Mrs Barry.'

Dejected, Mara allowed the older girl to take her by the arm. She couldn't even be bothered to resist.

'And Alison – '

'Yes?'

'When Mara's gang get back from the town, please tell them to come and see me at once. As soon as they've put their bikes away.'

'And this girl who was kidnapped – Linda Grigoris – is Mara's cousin?' exclaimed Rebecca. 'I don't remember reading about it in the papers.'

She remembered Mara's mysterious reference to 'the

Grigoris affair' in her letter and had been meaning to ask her about it. Now she understood.

'There've been so many kidnappings on that particular holiday island in the last few years,' commented Mrs Barrington. 'It only made a few lines. Linda was spending Christmas there with her family and the bandits took her from the garden of their holiday villa in broad daylight and up into the mountains. She was released, completely unharmed, after six days. Mr Grigoris paid quite a hefty ransom, one gathers.'

'So what,' said Tish.

Mrs Barrington glanced round at the five girls, uneasily. They were all seated in her private sittingroom. She was a little perturbed by their rebellious attitude.

'Now, listen, girls, I want you to take this seriously. Mara is very lucky to have been allowed back to Trebizon this term. She's lucky to be here at all! Her father wanted to keep her in Athens, but Miss Welbeck had a long telephone conversation with him last week and they've come to this arrangement. She also had a chat with Mara's brother, when he brought her back to school this afternoon.'

So that's why they went over to the main building first, thought Rebecca.

'What arrangement?' asked Margot.

'You know perfectly well,' said Mrs Barrington. 'You're not trying to pretend to me that Mara hasn't explained it to you?'

The girls were silent, their expressions giving nothing away. They had no intention of getting Mara into any more trouble. But they listened.

44

'Let me spell it out quite clearly, just to make sure. Mara is confined to school.'

The others didn't move a muscle but Rebecca and Tish exchanged startled glances. The truth was out – the truth that Mara had tried to hide from them! Of course, they'd begun to suspect this stongly, but it was still a shock to have it confirmed.

'It's not fair!' Rebecca cried. 'It's like being a junior again!'

'It's stupid,' said Elf.

'Come, come.' The house mistress was striving to keep on top of the situation. 'It's not as bad as all that. She's not allowed to go out *on her own*. But, after all, if there's anything she *really* wants to do, she only has to phone Mr Papaconstantopoulos at the Trebizon Bay Hotel and he'll come and take her by car and stay with her and bring her back. . . .'

Tish just laughed out loud. 'S ne hopes of her wanting to do that!'

'That's enough,' said the house mistress sharply. 'I don't want to discuss it further. Kindly see that there's no repetition of tonight's behaviour and do all you can to help Mara obey her father's instructions.'

She dismissed them.

As soon as they'd gone, she telephoned the principal at her house in the school grounds.

'Madeleine, this Leonodis business is going to be a real headache. Mara's friends think the whole thing is quite silly.'

'So do I,' said Miss Welbeck. 'But we're just going to have to make the best of things and hope it blows over.'

45

When the friends were back in the boarding house, they went straight to the room to see Mara, but she wasn't there. They stood around her bed talking, the door wide open. Across the corridor, the opposite door opened and Lucy Hubbard came out, jingling some money.

'Mara's night things have gone – and her shower cap,' said Margot.

'She must be getting ready for bed,' added Elf.

'Let's wait for her here then,' said Rebecca. 'At least we've got the whole picture now. Poor Mara! She must be feeling depressed!'

They were talking loudly and Lucy could hear them.

'Fancy Mara not telling us everything,' mused Sue. 'About her cousin being kidnapped and how she's not supposed to go out – '

'But can you blame her?' said Tish and Rebecca nodded in agreement. 'She decided to break out and she wanted to take the whole thing on her own shoulders and not involve us!'

'Maybe we should have guessed,' said Rebecca.

Lucy Hubbard suddenly appeared in the doorway. She looked smaller than ever in pyjamas and dressing gown. She was obviously bursting to speak to them.

'*I* guessed!' she said. 'I read about her cousin in *The Times* and I realised who she was the minute she arrived, and why she needed a bodyguard.'

'*The Times* – get that,' said Elf, in an aside.

'None of us can read at Trebizon,' explained Sue, acidly. 'All our text books are in picture strips.'

'Nonsense!' said Lucy, just like a miniature grown up.

46

'There are some specially gifted girls at this school. That's why I've been brought here...'

'Coo!'

'Cor!'

'...you see Mummy says my last school didn't *stretch* me enough.'

'If you go around talking like that,' said Rebecca, gently, suddenly feeling almost sorry for the girl, 'you'll get stretched all right – on a rack or something.'

Directness was Tish's style.

'Why don't you shut up and stop showing off and mind your own business?'

'I'm not showing off!' protested Lucy. 'I *did* guess about your friend and it's fortunate I did. And it's fortunate I answered the telephone when her brother rang up! Otherwise – ' Her eyes grew big and round. 'Well, just think, she might have been kidnapped by now.'

The friends all gazed at her incredulously and then exchanged despairing looks with one another. Tish was the first to recover. She walked over to the door and closed it gently, but firmly, in Lucy's face.

'Off you go! Night, night. Time for beddy-byes!'

Then they started to laugh. They just couldn't help it.

'How can somebody who's supposed to be so clever be so *stupid?*' asked Sue.

'She's just a baby, if you ask me,' said Rebecca.

Out in the corridor, Lucy could hear them laughing. She was completely baffled. Didn't they realise how dangerous it was for their friend to be wandering around the town in the dark, without any grown-ups? Was that all the thanks she got?

She didn't think she was going to like it at Trebizon.

She'd been hoping all evening that the 'phone would ring and she was on her way there now, some coins in her dressing gown pocket. Mummy had forbidden her, but she wouldn't think about that now. Mummy kept telling her how much she was going to like it here, but blow that!

She reached the coinbox 'phone under the stairs and lifted the receiver. She started to dial, money at the ready. She'd get about six minutes and then could be rung back.

It would be lovely just to talk to him!

4
Mara Cheers Up

Alison Hissup brought Mara back, all clean and
scrubbed in a dressing gown, and dumped her in the
room with her friends.

'Mrs Barry says she's got to get to bed early!' she shot at them and then fled. She'd already missed half her favourite TV show!

'Mara!' They tried to surround her, but she broke free.

She burst into tears and flung herself down on the bed, face in the pillow, a fist pummelling the sheet.

'I'll never be able to go into Fenners again! I was the laughing stock! It was...humiliating!' She sobbed some more. 'I hate my father. I hate Anestis. Most of all, I hate Papa – '

Tish and Margot sat on the bed and tried to sooth her while the others stood around helplessly.

'It's *stupid* – '

'Ridiculous!'

That only sent Mara off into fresh spasms. Her legs kicked.

'All the lovely things Curly's been planning...oh! He won't want anything to do with me now! He'll keep clear of me by miles! He'll cut me dead!'

'Of *course* he won't, Mara!' protested Rebecca.

'He's going to 'phone you!' added Sue. 'He said so!'

'He won't! I just know he won't!'

As Mara broke into more noisy sobs, the others conferred in whispers.

'Shall we leave her to have a good cry? She'll feel better then.'

'Let's all go and get ready for bed and then come back – '

'We can bring the rest of the fudge!'

As soon as they were out of the room, Sue said:

'I know! I'll ring Syon and see if Mike's back

50

yet.' Syon House was the name of the boys' boarding house at Garth College. 'I'll tell him everything! He can get Curly to ring Mara straight back – tonight – '

'Great idea!'

'I think I'll wash my hair while I'm in the shower,' said Rebecca. 'It's filthy.'

Later, when she was in the shower room in her dressing gown, just towelling her hair dry, Sue came rushing through.

'Wait for me, Rebecca. Hold my glasses.'

She dived into one of the shower cubicles.

'Did you get Mike?' called Rebecca.

'Yes!' There was the noise of water running and Rebecca could see steam rising. 'And guess what, Curly's rung back already and Mara's talking to him right now. I even heard her laughing!'

'Thank goodness!' said Rebecca, relieved. 'Where are the others?'

'In the room in their dressing gowns, with the fudge, waiting for her.'

By the time Rebecca and Sue got along there, Mara was back from the 'phone and sitting on the bed eating fudge with the others. In the space of twenty minutes, all her tears had changed to smiles.

'Have you two forgiven me, too?' she asked.

'Forgiven you?' began Rebecca.

'I should have *told* you I was forbidden to go down town!' said Mara in a rush. 'But I couldn't! You might have stopped me coming!'

'Oh, *that*,' shrugged Sue.

'I got you into trouble with Mrs Barry,' said Mara. 'I'm sorry.'

'We just told her what we thought of the whole idea,' said Rebecca, loyally. 'Honestly! Treating you as a junior again, just because of something that happened to your cousin! It's not fair!'

'My father is crazy,' agreed Mara.

For a moment her dark eyes smouldered and she nodded in the direction of the door, thinking of the new girl in the room opposite.

'That girl – Lucy Hubbard – she gave me away! She's the one who should be treated as a junior. That's all she is! *She's* the one who needs looking after, isn't she, Sue?'

'Why's that?' asked Rebecca, surprised.

'She's been ringing up boys!' explained Elf. 'Sue heard her on the 'phone – tell Rebecca, Sue.'

'Oh, yes, I could hardly believe my ears!' said Sue. It had been while she'd been waiting to 'phone Mike Brown. 'Kiss, kiss, into the 'phone – "I love you, too" – all that sort of thing.'

'Well, it's a free country!' laughed Rebecca. 'I wonder if he's still in short trousers?'

'Probably. And I expect they do *The Times* crossword together,' said Sue.

'All the same, I bet her mother wouldn't approve,' said Mara darkly.

Elf handed some more fudge round and they let it melt in their mouths. Mara's smouldering look had gone and a happy, dreamy expression had taken its place. Tish looked at her, full of curiosity.

'Er – how was Curly, then?' she asked.

'Oh, he's nice,' said Mara happily. 'He knows exactly how to cheer somebody up! He said there was nothing to get upset about – in fact he laughed and laughed and somehow that made me laugh, too.'

'There!' said Margot, relieved.

'He's promised to come and visit me here, at weekends!' added Mara. 'Oh, he's so funny!' She smiled, remembering. 'He said, why don't I go on the float anyway, when they've built it, and he'll arrange for a couple of boys to kidnap me! It'd get in the newspapers – the most wonderful publicity stunt for the Concert – '

'Typical Curly!' said Tish, with that big grin of hers.

'I wish I dared!' Mara clapped her hands and laughed excitedly. 'Just imagine Papa scurrying here, there and everywhere, thinking I'd been kidnapped – wouldn't that just serve him right? And my father!'

It was a lovely idea. Ridiculous, but lovely.

They all started to laugh. Nobody heard a creak outside the door. Lucy Hubbard, coming back from cleaning her teeth, had paused to listen. She crept away to her room, shocked.

Later, Rebecca, Tish and Sue went to their room too. They talked in sleepy whispers as they lay in bed.

'Well, Mara seems happy again,' said Rebecca.

'Very,' agreed Sue. 'She didn't even mention the disco! I can't see her wanting to take Papa to that! So that means she can't go. And the travelling float – that's out, too. Papa would never agree to that!'

'Unless he could sit up on the float beside her – ' giggled Rebecca.

'Dressed as a Red Indian, maybe!' added Tish.

Rebecca's eyelids felt heavier and heavier. It had been a long day. Tomorrow, the term – and lessons – would start in earnest.

The amazing things that happened! Poor Mara, coming back to school with her own personal bodyguard. Forbidden to go anywhere without him! But Mara was happy again because Curly still liked her. He'd promised to come and visit her at Court House. Some boys might have been put off by the whole situation, but not Curly.

Mara was going to miss out, though. It was a shame.

'I hope the boys do raise enough money to build the float,' said Rebecca drowsily. 'I've got something I can wear!' She'd remembered an Arabian costume that her mother had brought back from Saudi Arabia last year. The genuine article! She'd said Rebecca could have it and it was in a cupboard at her grandmother's. She must write and ask Gran to send it. 'I want to go on that float. I think it sounds really good fun.'

'Well, we'd better start selling those disco tickets tomorrow!' said Tish. She yawned loudly. 'Let's shut up and go to sleep now.'

And they did.

The next morning the six friends raced along the footpaths, crunching the overnight frost as they ran. They got to the Dining Hall early. They wanted to bag places at their favourite table – Joss Vining's – before Mrs Hubbard came and plonked Lucy amongst them again!

They made it. Now they would be safe the rest of the term.

Tish watched Lucy's mother bring her into the hall, soon afterwards, rooting around for a table with some III Alpha girls on it. She managed to squeeze her in with Debbie Rickard and the Nathan twins, on the next door table.

'I still think she'd be happier on one of the junior tables,' said Tish, with a shrug. 'She's only their age – even if she is Miss Brain of Britain – so she'd get on with them better.'

'And she's really in Court House?' said Joss, in surprise. 'And our form, too?' As they all nodded, she looked Lucy over. 'Hmmm.'

'No good for the hockey or netball teams?' said Tish. 'Is that what you're thinking?' Joss was a brilliant all-round athlete and Head of Games in the Third Year.

Joss laughed and shook her head.

'I was thinking about the Gymnastics Club that Miss Willis is going to start this term. She could join that. She's exactly the right build.'

'Oh, Joss!' grumbled Elf. 'Is nobody safe when you're around?'

'Gym Club?' asked Rebecca. That sounded interesting!

'Forget it, Rebeck,' said Tish quickly. She poured some milk on her cereal for her. 'Tennis, remember.'

Rebecca didn't really need reminding. If she wanted to make it as a tennis player, when she'd started the game late, she had to be dedicated and she was.

'What I'm waiting to see,' said Mara, 'is whether she's

55

as clever as she's supposed to be.' She was gazing balefully across at Lucy Hubbard's back view. Last summer Mara had worked very hard to get herself put up into the Alpha stream, because she wanted to be with her friends. Getting into III Alpha had been such a triumph! Now this tiny little girl had come along and...well! 'Perhaps it's all a big mistake,' she added.

But it wasn't.

Lucy Hubbard, as the friends discovered during the course of the first week, seemed to be good at *everything*!

'How does she remember all those dates?' pondered Sue, after history lesson. 'It's indecent.'

'She's good at maths, too,' said Tish, wistfully. 'I don't think I'll be top in maths this term!'

In the staff room, Mrs Hubbard talked incessantly about her daughter.

'It's a very special *privilege* and *responsibility* to have given birth to a child like Lucy,' she told Miss Gates, the senior maths mistress.

Miss Gates made no comment, nor was she expected to. Her role was to listen. She carried on marking a pile of maths exercise books. At the same time, by just the correct inclination of the head, she gave all the appearance of listening carefully.

'You won't believe this, Miss Gates, but she was potty-trained by the time she was six months old...'

For Rebecca and her friends, only one thing alleviated the situation.

Although Lucy Hubbard was a very good pupil, her mother was a very bad teacher. For one thing, she continually singled out her own daughter for special

56

praise, although Lucy was hardly the kind who needed a helping hand. For another thing, she couldn't keep order. The combination of the two made for great hilarity and excitement in geography.

'Well *done*, Lucy. That is one of the best answers I have been given to that particular question. A model answer in fact. I shall award you a special merit mark.'

'Hurray!' shouted Tish and led a mounting burst of applause and stamping of feet. Even the normally quiet ones joined in.

'Silence, please!' piped Mrs Hubbard. 'Don't be quite so noisy please girls.'

But the noise continued unabated. Lucy Hubbard was sitting in the front row next to Debbie Rickard and, even from the back row, Rebecca could see her neck slowly turning red, as she pretended to look through her atlas with great concentration.

'Three merit marks for Lucy in one week!' called someone. 'Hip, hip – '

'Please stop it, girls,' said Mrs Hubbard, getting flustered.

Then she produced a ploy.

'I shall leave the room. I shall be outside standing in the corridor. When you have calmed down and feel ready to proceed with the lesson, you may call me in.'

She was gone.

The form room rocked with laughter. Sue was almost hysterical. Rebecca was laughing so much her stomach ached.

'How many spins?' cried Tish, jumping up on to the teacher's dais with her hand poised to spin round the globe. 'Best guess gets a merit mark – '

'Sixteen!'

'Twenty three – '

'Twenty seven!'

Tish sent the globe spinning round and round. They all started counting in unison, at the tops of their voices:

'...SEVEN...EIGHT...NINE...TEN... ELEVEN...'

Rebecca caught a glimpse of Lucy's face, turned towards the spinning globe. She was captivated by the game, joining in loudly with the rest of them.

'...NINETEEN...NINETEEN-AND-A-HALF...'

'I've won!' cried Jenny Brook-Hayes.

Mrs Hubbard, standing out in the corridor, was quite forgotten.

In the end there was a loud knock, a clearing of the throat outside the door – 'Ready now, girls?' – and she came back into the room to resume the lesson.

The first Saturday of term turned out to be a full day for the six, in different ways. It didn't leave time to think about Lucy Hubbard, or even to notice her very much. She appeared to spend most of the day in her mother's company.

Mara was as happy as a lark at breakfast, her hair freshly washed and eyes bright. She planned to spend the morning doing extra study in the library, for she was determined to keep her place in III Alpha. Curly was coming in the afternoon. They were going swimming together in the heated pool at the school sports centre.

Sue was excited. She had orchestra practice and apparently Mr Barrington was going to choose some of them for a special Joint Orchestra that would take part in the ICF Concert at Garth College at half-term. 'Imagine mixing with some of the famous stars that are going to be in the concert!' exclaimed Sue. 'Oh, I do hope I'm chosen!'

Elf, to her delight, had suddenly been given a day's exeat because her uncle, who lived in Australia, and was visiting England, had telephoned to ask if he could take her to a theatre matinee in Exonford.

Rebecca, Margot and Tish wanted to go down town and look round the shops at clothes. It was rather cold though, and snowing again. It was Tish who had the marvellous idea.

'What d'you think Papa's doing?' she asked Mara, as she spread marmalade on her toast. 'It must be terribly boring for him sitting round the Trebizon Bay Hotel every day.'

'I don't care what he's doing!' said Mara happily. 'The more bored he gets, the better! He can telephone my father and tell him there is nothing for him to do here and then perhaps he'll be called back to Athens. Personally I wouldn't be seen dead with him!'

'You know full well he isn't going to be called back to Athens,' said Tish, through a mouthful of toast. She was grinning. 'It seems a shame not to make use of him -'

'I mean, your father's paying him!' said Rebecca, suddenly cottoning on. 'It seems an awful waste - '

'*We* wouldn't mind being seen with him!' finished Margot. She glanced at some big snowflakes, whirling and tumbling down outside the window of the dining hall. 'Not if that car's cosy and warm!'

'What a fantastically good idea!' exclaimed Mara. She laughed and clapped her hands. 'I shall 'phone him straight after breakfast and tell him to put himself and the car at your disposal. Yes!' She laughed again. 'This will be even better than his being bored. Let us make his life a little irksome!'

The morning must indeed have been a little irksome for the big Greek, driving three of Mara's friends from shop to shop. Parking spaces were few and far between, for Saturday morning was busy, the town full of people from outlying villages. The big unwieldly car was not designed for easy parking.

Papa was baffled that they could never seem to find what they were looking for. They would spend anything up to half an hour in a clothes shop and yet still come out empty-handed, laughing quite happily.

He never dreamt that they had no money on them, but were simply having a wonderful time trying on clothes. Tish and Margot planned what they'd wear to the disco, if only they'd had the money to buy it, while Rebecca tried on beautiful dresses just for the sheer joy of it.

It was the best fun they'd ever had in town! If Mr Papaconstantopoulos were at all irked, he remained quite unruffled, even when a traffic warden gave him a parking ticket. Finally, he drove them back to school in style, deposited them at the door of Court House and genially shook each of them by the hand in turn.

'Thank you, Papa.'

'My pleasure and thank you.'

At lunch time, Mara laughed about it until the tears ran down her cheeks. 'I shall ring him up whenever you want me to! Surely he will get fed up and tell father! Surely he will want to go home!'

'D'you think he'd drive me to Garth for the rehearsals?' joked Sue. She *had* been chosen for the Joint Orchestra that morning and was thrilled about it! 'I mean, I like going in the minibus but I hate taking my violin. I never know where to put it.'

'Then you shall go in the minibus and Papa can drive the violin to rehearsals!' said Mara. And the joking continued.

Rebecca enjoyed the afternoon as much as the morning, for the weather cleared up, the staff tennis court dried out and she and Joss Vining managed to get two hours very hard singles play in before dusk. Now that she was in the county 'D' squad she looked forward to travelling to Exonford on alternate Saturdays, again. It was only a week away now. She wondered how she was going to make out!

It wasn't until cocoa time that Lucy Hubbard impinged on Rebecca's thoughts. She found Anne Finch and Ann Ferguson had taken refuge in the kitchen because Lucy had already gone to bed.

'Her mother came and tucked her up with a teddy bear. We teased her afterwards and she started crying.'

'It's awful having to share a room with such a baby. But we feel a bit sorry for her really. I'd just hate Mother Hubbard to be my mother!'

Rebecca said nothing, but she felt a twinge of conscience. She'd started off the term feeling sorry for Mara. Now she wondered if she didn't feel more sorry for Lucy.

5
After the Disco

Rebecca asked herself that Saturday night if there were anything she could do to help Lucy Hubbard fit in better. She decided to try.

But in the course of the next seven days her sympathies were to swing right away from Lucy and back to Mara – and what happened after the disco was the last straw.

However on Sunday morning, directly after church, she marched Lucy along to the Sports Centre. The meeting to form a Gymnastics Club was taking place at 11.30. Miss Welbeck had announced it in assembly on Friday.

'I don't want to join a silly club, it's childish,' protested Lucy, who never seemed to think of herself as a child. 'There's a book on 18th century country houses in the library and I want to study it – '

'Just come and find out about it,' said Rebecca firmly.

'I'm very interested in the infrastructure of the Trebizon estate. I think the nobleman who built Trebizon may well have created a grotto somewhere – '

'So what,' said Rebecca. Though, thinking about it later, it seemed quite an interesting idea. 'You can read the book up this afternoon.'

About twenty girls had turned up to find out about the Gym Club, mainly First Years and Second Years. They seemed very excited about it. Rebecca asked Eleanor Keating and Sheila Cummings to look after Lucy and then she left.

'What were you doing with *her*?' asked Mara as Rebecca joined her on the touchline at North hockey pitch. Even in their warm capes they shivered a little, but there was a team practice match going on between the First and Second Elevens and it was worth watching, especially now Tish was in the Second Eleven. 'Did you see the way Tish got the ball then!'

'I was only taking her over to Gym Club,' said Rebecca, slightly embarrassed. 'If she could get interested in things and make some friends her own age, she mightn't be such a pain in the neck.'

'You are very charitable, Rebecca,' said Mara. Then, characteristically her face lit up and she gave Rebecca a sudden, warm hug. 'Oh, Rebecca, you are much too charitable! I must try and be as charitable as you!'

But it wasn't easy being charitable.

Just before Sunday lunch, Rebecca was pounding a tennis ball against the wall of Norris and thinking about Joss Vining. She knew how lucky she was to have a player like Joss in the school, a fully-fledged 'A' squad county junior who'd even competed at Junior Wimbledon! She only had to play against her to realise what a lot she had still to learn. She wished they could have played again this morning, but right now Joss was taking part in the hockey practice – the youngest girl ever to be picked for Trebizon's First Eleven. She was a sports prodigy but surely, thought Rebecca, sooner or later Joss would have to make her choice...

She was thinking these thoughts when the two Annes came by.

'Whatever's wrong?' she asked, looking at their faces.

'Lucy sneaked on us!' said Anne Finch.

'Mother Hubbard's just given us a lecture,' explained Ann Ferguson. 'She wasn't meek and mild like she usually is. She was in the most filthy temper – '

'When we got there – ' Anne took up the story, ' – she was on the 'phone having a terrible quarrel with somebody, we heard her. It was something about the Sunday dinner of all things! Then she slammed the 'phone down when we arrived and vented all her bad temper on us.'

'She's sending us to see Miss Welbeck in the morning. It's not *fair*. It's the first time we've ever teased Lucy and we weren't going to do it again.'

'Spoilt little baby!'

Rebecca bit her lip and said nothing. Instead, she caught Lucy as soon as she arrived back at Court and pulled her into the common room, which was empty.

'I've decided I shall probably join the Gym Club,' Lucy began importantly. 'If that's what you want to know – '

'Why did you sneak to your mother about the two Annes?'

Lucy looked surprised. She was totally oblivious of Rebecca's anger.

'I always tell Mummy everything. She expects me to.'

The first dinner bell went and Rebecca gave up. What a hopeless case!

Mara had enjoyed her Saturday afternoon with Curly and she began the new week quite cheerfully. But as the days passed and talk began to turn to the disco at the weekend, she gradually grew more despondent.

To make matters worse she was having some problems with her maths and Miss Hort had given her a lot of extra work to do. Rebecca was much too excited about going to Exonford to care about missing the disco herself, but she began to feel sorry for Mara all over again.

They'd sold all their tickets easily and Curly had cycled over with some more on Wednesday. Nearly all the Third and Fourth Years in Court House were going and a lot from the other middle school houses as well. The Fifth Years remained aloof, but then they were working hard for their mock exams.

'Like my brother Edward is,' Sue said, discussing it in bed one night. 'Is Robbie?'

'Must be. Hasn't once been to see Virginia Slade,' replied Tish.

Rebecca had been wondering about that.

'Well, you don't need the Fifth Years,' she said lightly. 'It looks like being a sell-out.'

On Friday evening, while the others discussed what they would wear to the disco, Mara sat in the other room and struggled with her maths.

But at cocoa time she came into the kitchen, looking quite pleased with herself.

'Tish, I love you!' she said. Tish had been helping her, earlier. 'At last I see how to do them! Tomorrow night, when you all go off and enjoy yourself at the disco, I shall lock myself in the room and copy everything into my best book.'

They all made a fuss of Mara then, for putting such a brave face on things.

And the situation certainly had its compensations. Papa was taking Rebecca to Exonford, in the big car! Mara insisted on it. It wasn't the first time she'd made the point –

'Myself I'm ashamed of him. I would be the complete laughing stock if I let him take me anywhere. He would follow me around all the time and spy on me!

'But for you, Rebecca, it is quite different. Let us use silly Papa and that silly car!'

Rebecca felt very grand, stepping into the big car on Saturday, straight after lunch. Papa held open the door for her and then took her sports bag and tennis racket and put them in the boot. Windows opened all over Court House and girls stuck their heads out, laughing and waving.

'Have a great time at the disco!' Rebecca called to Tish & Co. 'Tell Mara not to work too hard!'

With a contented sigh she sank into the deep leather upholstery and the car rolled away. This was even more fun than going on the train! Less than an hour later the flags of the big modern sports centre at Exonford came in view.

Rebecca's first afternoon's tennis training with the 'D' squad was a great success. She knew Toby from the reserve squad, as they'd been promoted together at Christmas. The other six members of the squad, three boys and three girls, seemed very friendly and so did the coach, whose name was Mrs Ericson.

They all worked very hard and Rebecca felt she'd done quite well. They were joined at tea-time by various officials and senior tennis players, as well as some local businessmen who sponsored county tennis. A social gathering followed and the day ended with a film showing the highlights of the previous year's Wimbledon Championships.

Rebecca felt shy amongst so many adults and enjoyed the film part most of all. As Papa drove her back to school along the dark roads, she day-dreamed of playing on the Centre Court one day in the distant future – Rebecca Mason, tennis star!

Papa deposited her at the front door of the boarding house and she thanked him and went inside. For a moment she wondered why it was silent and deserted on a Saturday evening, usually such a noisy time with records playing and the television blaring. Then she remembered!

'Of course, everyone's gone to the disco! The coach must have collected them at least an hour ago!'

But Mara would be here.

Rebecca went and threw her sports bag and tennis racket on to her bed and called 'Mara!'

The door of the room opposite opened. Not quite everyone had gone to the disco. Lucy Hubbard stood there. She was putting her finger to her lips.

'Ssssh!'

'What?'

Lucy pointed to Mara's door. It was firmly shut and a sign was hanging from the door handle: DO NOT DISTURB.

'She's got a headache,' whispered Lucy. 'She's only come out of the room once this evening, that was when the 'phone rang – but it was for me. After I came off the 'phone she looked out and told me that no-one must disturb her because she was trying to do her maths and her head was aching.'

'Oh, poor thing,' said Rebecca. She thought: 'But I'm not Lucy.'

She took the few steps to Mara's door, opened it and looked inside –

'Hi, Mara – '

Rebecca froze.

The room was empty. A tell-tale breeze from the big sash window fluttered the pages of a maths text book that lay open on the homework table. Open where Mara had left it.

The window wasn't shut properly at the bottom. Rebecca remembered that it was stiff and difficult to close from the inside. From the outside, impossible.

Mara had gone somewhere – via the window.

Mara had gone to the disco!

'Is she all right?' piped Lucy's voice, just a few feet away.

Rebecca's mind worked rapidly.

'Hey, Mara, are you asleep or something?' she said to the empty room.

She paused, to allow time for a reply.

'Okay,' she said then. 'Sure you don't want anything? Right, see you then!'

Rebecca then carefully closed the door, her heart banging hard. She turned to face Lucy in the corridor and now it was her turn to put her finger to her lips.

'She's not asleep, but she's lying down,' she whispered. 'You were right. We musn't disturb her!'

Lucy nodded solemnly and went back inside her own room.

Rebecca hurried along to the kitchen to make herself some coffee, almost doubled up with the desire to laugh after the sheer tension of the last couple of minutes.

As soon as she'd drunk her coffee, she took a torch and slipped out to the cycle sheds. She flashed her torch along the row.

'My bike!' she realised. 'She's gone to the disco on *my* bike!'

For a while after that, Rebecca found it impossible to relax.

She lay on top of her bed, reading a book, at the same time keeping her ears attuned to the corridor. Supposing Lucy was suspicious? Supposing she decided to go and look in Mara's room.

But everything was silent in their little corridor and Rebecca's eyelids began to get heavy. She'd enjoyed every minute of the tennis training, but it had been quite exhausting...

As for Mara...!

She dozed off.

Sometime later she suddenly awoke. What was that noise? A shuffling sound – footsteps shuffling past her open door!

She jumped off the bed and shot into the corridor. Just in time to see a small figure in dressing gown and carpet slippers opening the door of Mara's room –

'Lucy!' she yelled.

'I've made her some cocoa – ' whispered Lucy.

Rebecca hurtled up to Lucy and tried to pull her back, but she was already inside the room, staring all around, looking blank, the steaming mug of cocoa in her hand.

'Where is she – ?'

'I was trying to tell you,' Rebecca began desperately. 'She – went to have a shower or something, I mean...'

Suddenly Lucy screamed.

The window was opening and a ghostly leg came over the sill.

Then a body and head followed and Lucy realised it was Mara, wearing white cord trousers and a white velvet jacket.

'Rebecca!' cried Mara. She was out of breath from her cycle ride but she looked elated. She'd obviously had a marvellous time. 'I've been a very bad girl, haven't I – '

Then, getting used to the bright light indoors, she saw Lucy.

'Oh, *no*,' she groaned.

They were all immobilized.

Then, hand shaking a little, Lucy put the cocoa down and backed slowly, very slowly, out of the room. She was deeply shocked.

'You could have been kidnapped!' she cried at last.

Oh, Lucy, look –' began Rebecca. 'For heaven's sake –'

But Lucy had already fled along the corridor and across the main hall. Mara and Rebecca could hear her hammering loudly on Mrs Barrington's door. They didn't know whether to laugh or cry.

'We've had a marvellous time, Mrs Barry!' exclaimed Tish, first off the coach. 'The boys raised £100 tonight and –'

The house mistress was waiting outside the front porch with her coat on and her arms folded. The porch light cast her face in shadow.

'Then you can tell the Principal all about it,' she said. 'At ten tomorrow morning. She wants to see the whole gang of you and she's rather displeased, I can tell you.'

6
Seeing Miss Welbeck

'I knew she'd never get away with it!' said Margaret
Exton, cleaning her teeth in the Fourth Year washroom
upstairs. 'Somebody was bound to split!'

'I expect it was old Slade,' said Sarah Turner, squeezing a fat splodge of fluoride toothpaste on her brush. 'Must be round the boys' school by now that Mara Leonodis is supposed to go everywhere with her male nurse!'

Mr Slade was Curly's housemaster at Garth College. He'd been in charge of the disco that evening.

'I shouldn't think so,' said Moyra Milton. 'I wonder who did split? I think it's a shame. I loved it when she went up with the band and sang those Greek songs. She's got a marvellous singing voice!'

'She certainly enjoyed herself! Not a care in the world!'

'Did you see Mrs Barry's face when we got back?' asked Margaret Exton, not without some satisfaction. 'It was like a thundercloud!'

'Oh, shove over and let's have the basin, Maggie.'

Court House was agog.

Downstairs, Mara had already been sent to bed in disgrace and soon the other five were in their pyjamas, too, looking woebegone as they crowded round her bed.

'I'll tell Miss Welbeck you all had nothing to do with it!' Mara said rebelliously. 'Why should you get into trouble for something you didn't even know anything about?'

'Oh, it's not that – ' said Tish.

'It's just a rotten end to the evening,' said Sue. 'Wasn't Chris fantastic on trumpet?'

'We really thought you'd got away with it!' said Elf.

'And I would have done, too!' said Mara, sending dark looks through the wall at Lucy Hubbard's room across the corridor. Then she glanced at Rebecca. 'Sorry about

74

borrowing your bike. It's good, isn't it!'

Suddenly they heard Mrs Barrington's voice calling on the main staircase. *Stop all this noise, everybody. Come on, lights out!*

They scattered. Margot and Elf jumped to their beds and the other three shot out of the door – 'See you in the morning!' – and into their own room. They didn't put the light on, but scrambled to their beds in the darkness. It was really rather late.

'Isn't Mara a dark horse?' Rebecca said then. 'I can't get over it! Did you guess she was planning to – '

'But she wasn't!' whispered Tish. 'She was sitting doing her maths as good as gold. She told us all about it. All she was counting on was a 'phone call from Curly – he'd promised. Then the 'phone rang – '

' – but the 'phone call was for Lucy Hubbard, not her,' finished Sue. 'This boy back home or whoever it is who keeps ringing her. Mara was livid to think that even little Lucy was having more fun than she was.'

'So – it was spur of the moment!' said Rebecca.

'Completely! It was all Curly's fault for not ringing!'

'He was wearing some new cords and they were so tight, they split!' Sue explained. 'While they were getting the hut ready. By the time he'd got back to Syon and found someone to borrow trousers from – David, in fact – it was too late to ring Mara – he was supposed to be on the drums!'

David was Sue's other brother, and he was almost as short as Curly, although he was a year older.

'What on earth did David wear to the disco then?' whispered Rebecca.

'He didn't!'

'What?'

'I mean he didn't go to the disco, you fool!'

They started to giggle helplessly, until the sound of Mrs Barrington's footsteps outside forced them to be quiet and go to sleep.

There was no giggling next morning when the six of them assembled in front of Miss Welbeck. As it was Sunday, she'd asked them to come to her private house in the school grounds. None of them had ever been sent for on a Sunday before.

'I'm quite prepared to accept that your friends didn't actively encourage you in this, Mara,' the Principal said gently. 'But I want to talk to you and it will do no harm for them to listen to what I have to say. It's most important that they try to help you to keep to the arrangements that I've made with your father for the rest of this term – '

She then went on to repeat what the arrangements were and to point out that Mara was free to go anywhere she wanted to as long as she made sure that Mr Papaconstantopoulos accompanied her at all times.

'I quite understand that you may find this arrangement embarrassing and that it makes you feel self-conscious. But it won't last for ever. I shall do my best to see to that. We must give your father time to get over his anxieties about you and agree to let you have the freedom that as a member of the middle school you have the right to espect.'

'But it's not fair!' protested Rebecca. 'Just because Mara's cousin – '

'Life isn't always fair, Rebecca,' replied Miss Welbeck. 'It would have been even less fair if Mara had been forced to stay behind in Athens this term, but fortunately I was able to talk Mr Leonodis out of that course of action.' She paused. 'Mara's first duty is to her family and to her father, who is the head of that family. I want you all to understand that and to help her to understand it, too. You may go.'

They walked back across the school grounds, very subdued.

'Phew!' said Tish, at last.

Mara said nothing. She looked tearful. She'd enjoyed last night so much – she'd never enjoyed herself more in her life! But now she felt stymied. The trouble with Miss Welbeck was that she was so fair – so reasonable! She made you feel she was on your side and yet, at the same time –

'I've a good mind to run away!' Mara burst out at last. 'I'll run away from Trebizon! That would give him a shock! That would make him sorry!'

'Come off it, Mara.'

'Don't be stupid!'

They all gathered round her protectively.

'I know what!' said Tish. 'Those songs you were singing last night. Let's get them on tape. Sue can accompany you on the violin. Come on, it'll be fun. We can give the cassette to Curly, he'd like that.'

'Yes, please do,' said Rebecca. 'I mean to say, I haven't heard them yet. I didn't even *go* to the disco.'

'Ah, poor Rebecca,' said Mara, quite forgetting her anger for a moment.

'You missed a lot of fun.'

'She certainly did,' said Tish.

Mara looked at them and made a face.

'You are humouring me,' she said, after a while, 'but -, oh, all right. I shall stop being stupid.'

They spent the rest of Sunday morning making the tape. They all enjoyed themselves, Mara included.

'I think she's accepted the situation, don't you?' Sue said at lunch time, talking out of the corner of her mouth.

'That's her third of treacle sponge,' said Rebecca.

'I think,' said Tish, 'that everything's going to be all right.'

Everything might have been all right if Mara hadn't seen the float, or tried on Rebecca's costume. But she did. Even so -

It might still have been all right if Joss hadn't dropped her bombshell.

7
At Tennis Training

For two whole weeks after the interview with Miss Welbeck, Mara was a model of good behaviour. She still refused to have anything to do with Papa or let him take her anywhere. It was bad enough having to put up with jokes about her 'male nurse' as it was.

Keeping rigidly to bounds herself, she derived a certain amount of satisfaction from putting the car at her friends' disposal whenever they needed it. They used it mainly to go over to Garth College.

Sue had to go quite frequently because the Joint Orchestra was now rehearsing hard for the ICF Concert. Chris Earl-Smith had also got into the orchestra. He and Sue were its two youngest members.

The others went as often as they could manage it, because the boys needed help. Building scenery, a bandstand and, of course, the ticket office was a big job. And it all had to be designed to fit on the back of the lorry. It was fun watching everything take shape, helping to paint it all in brilliant colours. They gave Mara a full report each time and made sketches and diagrams, so that she could picture exactly what was happening and what the finished float would look like. Mara herself had designed a fine banner to go on the float, and was allowed to work on it in the art room: BUY YOUR TICKETS HERE FOR THE INTERNATIONAL CONCERT!

She felt very left out of things that fortnight, though. Curly couldn't come and see her. He was much too busy. He telephoned when he could.

Secretly, he refused to accept the idea that Mara wouldn't be coming on the float. Rebecca realised that with full force the night they finished the ticket booth, over at the Garth College woodwork centre. The girls had just put the last touches of paint to it. It had smart red and white stripes, with the words BOX OFFICE lettered across it.

'I'm going to have Mara sitting in there, in Greek national costume, selling the tickets!' he said. 'That's been my plan from the beginning.'

'But Curly – ' began Rebecca.

He cut her off.

'Where there's a will there's a way,' he said solemnly. 'I've got the will, so you girls had better find the way!'

They weren't sure whether he was serious or not.

On the way back to Court House, in the back of the car, the four of them discussed the costumes they'd wear on the float. Sue wasn't with them. In fact she wouldn't be coming on the float anyway because of the Joint Orchestra.

Margot, whose family originated from the West Indies, was making a traditional costume in Mrs Dalzeil's class. Elf was borrowing a Japanese kimono. Tish was going as a Scottish Highlander and having her kilt sent down from home, while Rebecca was waiting for her grandmother to send the Arabian costume.

'It's beautiful,' she said. 'And very old. Of course, I should be dark really, not fair... I'm glad I haven't got tennis training on ticket-selling days... But I can't get over what Curly said!' Rebecca heaved a sigh. 'Do you know what I think? I think he planned the whole idea round Mara in the first place.'

They all felt sad.

'If only she didn't feel quite so ashamed of Papa,' whispered Tish, nodding towards the hulking back and gleaming bald crown in front of them. 'Even though she lets him take us to Garth, he's not allowed to drive us further than the gates, in case anybody sees him!'

The girls were beginning to get quite fond of the big Greek. He, for his part, had ceased to find Mara's demands on behalf of her friends at all irksome. Sitting around a cold English seaside town at the end of January wasn't his idea of fun and at least it gave him something to do.

During that fortnight, to cheer both themselves and Mara up, the friends made a big joke of the idea of Mara being kidnapped. They pretended to see kidnappers round every corner.

'Look, Mr Douglas is pointing a pen at Mara!' whispered Tish.

'It's not really a pen,' hissed Rebecca. 'It's got special darts in it! She'll go numb all over and then he'll kidnap her – '

'Mara,' said Mr Douglas, 'why haven't you handed in your chemistry prep?'

On the middle Sunday, first out of the church, Elf pretended to be really excited.

'Listen, you lot!' She came rushing back into the porch where Rebecca and Co. had just finished talking to the school chaplain. 'Quick!' she whispered. 'I've just seen a man hiding behind a tombstone!'

'A kidnapper!' said Mara, in glee.

'He's small, with rimless spectacles – '

'So small, he's invisible,' laughed Rebecca, as they came abreast of the big granite tombstone that Elf had pointed to.

'There was someone bending down there,' laughed Elf.

The path leading away from the church was crowded and the tombstone lay close to it.

'Really Elf!' said Sue. There were a few day girls at Trebizon and their parents occasionally came to church with them. 'Somebody's poor innocent father – '

'But why bending down behind the tombstone?' asked Mara mysteriously, still enjoying the joke.

'To tie his shoelace,' said Sue.

'No!' laughed Rebecca. 'He'd dropped his gun!'

Occasionally Lucy Hubbard heard them joking like this and she never ceased to wonder at it. How could they make fun of something so serious? Sometimes it filled her with an obscure sense of anger that they seemed to enjoy themselves so much. But she felt great satisfaction that Mara was no longer taking dangerous risks. At last she was doing what the adults told her to. A good thing, too!

None of the six could bring themselves to be friendly towards Lucy, after what had happened after the disco; not even Rebecca. But Rebecca noticed that she'd made one or two friends amongst the juniors since joining the Gym Club. She'd even seen her in Moffatt's one day.

On the second Saturday, Rebecca had tennis training again.

The girls weren't needed at Garth. Mr Slade was taking delivery of the hired lorry and the boys were going to get the float all set up. They'd promised to bring it to show the girls, the finished object, on the Sunday afternoon.

At Exonford, Rebecca had a conversation with her

coach, Mrs Ericson, that was going to have some bearing on her future.

She felt she'd done particularly well at training this time. She was in the middle of a growing spurt and her added height seemed to be making a real difference to her control. Her co-ordination was improving, too. Everything seemed to be coming together. To prove it, she'd had some singles with Joss during the week and managed to take some games off her. That had been really exciting.

Mrs Ericson seemed to be taking a special interest in Rebecca. She came and sat down at the table with her at tea-time.

'You show remarkable promise, Rebecca,' she said. 'You could go a long way, if you get the right competition.'

'Could – could I?' Rebecca's scalp started to tingle.

'What we can do for you here is limited,' Mrs Ericson explained. 'Coaching, yes. Putting you on the right lines. But after that, everything depends on competition. You think you're good – the best in your club, maybe, or your form, or even your school – and then you meet someone who's better and you realise how much further you've got to go – '

'I know!' exclaimed Rebecca. 'That's why I'm so lucky that Joss Vining's at Trebizon. She plays with me quite a lot now – '

Mrs Ericson seemed not to hear, but carried straight on.

'You've got to keep on pitting yourself against better people. That means tournaments. In this country an aspiring tennis player needs a lot of help – to be able to take part in those tournaments, to climb up the ladder. – '

Rebecca was hanging on to every word.

'That either means sponsors, or your family helping, or both,' the coach continued. She glanced at Rebecca. 'How are your family placed? Will they be in a position to help you later on, to drive you to tournaments – ?'

Some of Rebecca's excitement faded.

'Well, no. My parents are in Saudi Arabia. I've only got my grandmother here and she hasn't got a car – well, to be honest, she can't even drive.'

'I see.'

'But I've got Joss Vining!' Rebecca repeated, eagerly.

Mr Slade drove the decorated float up to the front of old building on Sunday afternoon. The well-rehearsed band was on the back, playing lustily. Girls swarmed round, Mara and the others to the forefront. It looked magnificent.

The band stopped playing and everybody laughed and talked. Somebody produced canned drinks and packets of biscuits.

At one stage, Miss Welbeck herself came over to inspect the float.

'And that's your banner, is it, Mara? Mrs Barrington told me about it. Well done. I should think the whole effort is going to sell a lot of tickets!'

Before he left, Curly managed to speak to Mara alone.

'Well?'

'It's beautiful,' whispered Mara.

'You know I've wanted you on it, right from the beginning. Sitting in the little box office – do you like it – ?'

Mara nodded, silently.

'Look, Mara,' he said urgently, 'we've got till next weekend. It goes like this. We drop leaflets round the area all week, to prepare the way. Get plenty of people used to the idea that they're going to buy tickets. After all, they cost a bomb! Then we take the float down town next Saturday and we start selling!'

He gripped her arm tightly.

'So you've got a week to think of something! Surely you can shake off that watchdog of yours somehow – '

'Watson!' called Mr Slade. 'Come on, hop on board. We're going.'

The band started playing and the lorry drove away.

Mara watched it go until it disappeared from sight. She looked hopeless somehow and Rebecca came and stood beside her, and put an arm round her shoulders.

The following Wednesday, after the best game of singles they'd ever had, Joss dropped her bombshell. At first Rebecca could hardly take it in.

They were letting themselves out of the gate of the staff tennis court and Rebecca could tell that Joss had really enjoyed the game. She remembered her conversation with Mrs Ericson the previous Saturday.

'We're beginning to have proper games now, aren't we? You've been very patient, Joss.' And then, gratefully: 'I'm lucky to have you.'

Joss stared at Rebecca. She suddenly looked conscience-stricken.

'I'm sorry,' she said.

'Sorry?'

'I'm probably leaving this term.'

'*Joss!*'

'It's almost certain. I'll know by the weekend. Please don't ask questions and please don't spread it around, not yet. Oh, Rebecca – '

The tall girl stuck her fingers in her short brown curly hair and rubbed her head, looking embarrassed.

'I'm sorry,' she said again.

They walked through the staff gardens and everything seemed blurred. Rebecca remembered passing somebody sitting on a seat who looked familiar and yet not familiar. Like somebody she'd seen in a dream.

When she got back to Court House, she found the others had all gone over to Garth College to help deliver leaflets. Wednesday was a half-day at both schools. But Mara was sitting on Rebecca's bed.

'A parcel's come for you. It must be your costume.'

Apathetically Rebecca opened up the brown paper parcel and took out the shimmering gossamer-like gown, the lovely veil.

'Don't look so miserable!' exclaimed Mara. 'That *you* should be miserable. Try it on! Try it on!'

Just to please Mara, Rebecca took off her track suit top and started to pull on the gown.

'I'll have to wear this white jumper under it, anyway. Or else I'd freeze to death on the float,' Rebecca murmured. 'Oh – '

She couldn't get it on!

It was too small! She'd grown so much since last year that suddenly it was quite impossible to get into it. Come to think of it, it had been rather a squeeze then. She didn't dare tug or pull or she might tear it –

'It's no use,' said Rebecca. 'Help me get it off. Gently – '

Mara obliged. 'Oh, what a shame!' she cried.

'It doesn't matter,' said Rebecca. Suddenly nothing mattered very much! Did Mrs Ericson know about Joss? Was that why she was asking those questions – ? Yes, she must have known! 'I'll soon find something else to wear,' she added.

'Rebecca – ?'

'Mmmm?'

'It's so beautiful. Could I – would you mind – ?'

'Of course not!' Rebecca was still feeling too stunned to mind about anything. 'Go ahead and try it on. I'd love to see you in it.'

Mara rushed off to change in her own room, where there was a full length mirror. Rebecca got on the bed and sat propped against the pillow. She put her hands behind her head and closed her eyes, thinking deeply about how much tennis had come to mean to her.

When her eyes opened again a beautiful Arab girl stood there, a shimmering vision in white, only her eyes visible, dark brown and luminous, above the half-veil.

'Mara!'

'It fits me perfectly!' whispered Mara. There was a tremble of excitement in her voice. 'I could go on the float, Rebecca. No-one would recognize me! Not in that

89

dark little ticket booth. *Please* lend it to me – please say you will!'

Rebecca didn't care. She was fed up! Why shouldn't Mara have some fun? It was all so stupid, anyway. Even Miss Welbeck thought it was stupid! If they planned the whole thing very carefully, they could probably get away with it...

'*Please* say yes, Rebecca.'

Their eyes met.

'Why not?' said Rebecca.

'I love you!' Mara hugged her with joy. 'I'll get it off now – straight away, before anyone sees. Oh, Rebecca, you're wonderful!'

Rebecca knew there was no going back now!

So that was how Mara went on the float, after all.

And disappeared.

8
Lucy Again

Rebecca and Mara hatched their plan carefully and they took a vow to keep it secret. Mara was frightened that the others might try and stop her. Rebecca had a different worry. If Mara got caught on Saturday there'd be a terrible row but, in her present mood, Rebecca couldn't care less. She'd given Mara her word and if it led to trouble she'd face the consequences! But she didn't want the others to be punished, too.

If they knew nothing about it, then nobody could blame them.

It wasn't easy keeping it secret, though.

'Rebecca! You look great!' exclaimed Tish later. 'Wherever did you get it?'

The other four had got back to Court House to find Rebecca dressed, from tip to toe, in Dutch national costume. The clogs on her feet and the white cap perched on top of her blonde head both added to her height, so that she looked tall, slender and very striking.

'The Sixth Form Dramatic Society had it!' said Mara happily. 'Pippa has lent it to us!'

Rebecca shot Mara a warning look for using that word 'us' and for sounding so happy. But the others noticed nothing.

'It's lovely!' sighed Elf. 'Oh, I shall look such a small dumpy Japanese beside you.'

'What about that Arabian costume though?' asked Sue, staring at Rebecca. 'Hasn't it turned up?'

'Useless,' said Rebecca quickly. 'Much too tight. Freezing as well.' She looked out of the window at the grey February sky. 'Brrrrrr.'

Frightened that Sue might ask more questions, she changed the subject quickly.

'What was it like delivering the leaflets – ?'

'Oh, terrific – ' began Margot.

This time it was Tish's turn to give a warning look – to Margot.

'I mean, it was all right,' amended Margot, 'but cold. Really cold.'

'You were lucky, Mara,' said Elf, trying to sound convincing. 'Being in the warm. You didn't miss much.'

They tried so hard to be tactful on these occasions; it was awful for Mara, being left out of everything. But for once Mara didn't seem to mind at all.

She seemed quite serene, with just the hint of a sparkle in her eyes.

'Mara's ill! Really ill!' exclaimed Elf, coming into the kitchen early on Saturday morning.

Rebecca and Tish were up, wearing jeans and cooking breakfast. The two of them, together with Elf and Margot, had been given permission to make themselves an early breakfast at Court House. This would enable them to dress up and be over at main school by half-past eight, when the float would be arriving. The plan was to 'set up the shop' and sell some tickets at Trebizon first, to start the ball rolling, before setting off in style for a hectic day of ticket selling in the town and surrounding villages.

'What's wrong with her?' asked Tish anxiously.

'I don't know!' said Elf. 'She got up and dressed when we did for some unknown reason – and then she suddenly started staggering about. She feels all hot and dizzy...Margot's looking after her!'

'Better go and tell Mrs Barry!' said Rebecca quickly.

A few minutes' later Mrs Barrington emerged from the

room, supporting Mara. The Greek girl had donned her school cape and was carrying a bag with her pyjamas and dressing gown sticking out of the top. Faces appeared at the doors along the little corridor.

'You all right, Mara?' asked Sue, sleepily. She wasn't going on the float because of rehearsals. 'What's the matter?'

Mara just shook her head and the house mistress answered for her.

'Don't fuss, Susan. She's a little feverish, that's all. Probably 'flu. There are six girls in Crockers already – let's hope it's not going to sweep through the school. Come on, Mara. Complete isolation, I'm afraid, until Matron sees what develops. She'll have you tucked up in no time!'

Mrs Barrington took Mara outside to where Hodkin, the school chauffeur, was waiting to drive them to the school's small sanitorium, nicknamed Crockers. Crockers was a modern, single-storey building of white brick set amongst trees, just off the school's main drive. It looked antiseptic outside and inside it smelled it. It contained several single-bedded rooms into which girls with any hint of infectious disease could be isolated for a while.

'Poor Mara!' exclaimed Jenny Brook-Hayes, as the car roared away outside. All the ground floor girls were now milling about in the corridor, discussing it. 'Didn't she look ill?'

'Terrible!' agreed Elizabeth Kendall, who shared with Jenny and Jane Bowen. 'She *must* have 'flu!'

'It could be psychosomatic,' declared Lucy Hubbard.

94

'Whatsersomatic?' said Ann Ferguson, in surprise.

Tish, Elf and Margot came round the corner from seeing Mara off, just in time to hear Lucy holding forth to an interested audience:

'It's all a question of interaction between mind and body. Mara must be feeling very depressed and angry this morning because her friends are dressing up and going on that float today and she can't go with them. Her mental state is interacting with her physical state – '

'You mean, she's *making* herself ill?' enquired Anne Finch.

Before Lucy could reply, Tish silenced her.

'Shut up. Before you make *me* ill.'

Rebecca had been in the kitchen the whole time, seeing to the bacon and eggs and now she looked out and yelled to the other three: 'Come on! Breakfast!'

'Did you hear what that little horror was saying about Mara?' exclaimed Tish angrily, as they joined Rebecca in the kitchen. 'She said she might be just bringing her illness on deliberately – '

'Because she's fed up about everything,' added Elf.

'What a cheek!' said Margot. 'As if things aren't bad enough for Mara! Just think of it – down with 'flu – while we all have a marvellous time!'

Rebecca turned her back to attend to the cooker. There were little shivers running up and down her spine. She spoke, without turning.

'Come on, we'd better have a huge breakfast. It's going to be cold on that float. Tish, you like your egg turned over, don't you?'

Tish raised her dark eyebrows in surprise.

'Rebeck. Don't you *care* about Mara? That's not like you.'

'You didn't even see her off!' said Margot reproachfully.

'Oh, it's not much fun having people fussing round you when you feel ill,' said Elf, springing to Rebecca's defence. 'And it's true. We need to stoke up with plenty of food or *we'll* all go down with something, too.'

'The only thing you'll ever go down with Elf,' began Tish. 'Is – '

'Bloat!' finished Rebecca and, suddenly unable to stop giggling, she served the breakfast with her hand shaking.

Tish stared at her thoughtfully. It wasn't that funny! Whatever had got into Rebecca this morning?

She soon found out, of course.

The boys had recruited a new trumpeter because Chris Earl-Smith, like Sue, was needed for rehearsals for the big concert. John Bates played at full blast as the float drew slowly away from the front of old building, amidst cheers. Staff members as well as girls waved the tickets they had been buying.

'Good luck!'

'Try and sell out in one day!'

'See you later!'

'See you down town!'

Curly Watson emerged from the smart red-and-white box office and, carefully keeping his balance on the moving float, crossed and mounted the small bandstand. He took up the beat of 'John Brown's Body' and drummed triumphantly.

'We've sold sixty, sixty tick...ets!' he sung, over and over again.

Tish, decked out in full highland costume and sitting down against the ticket office with Margot and Elf, was beginning to feel excited. But Curly's mood surprised her.

'He hardly listened – about Mara being ill,' she said to Elf.

'Just making the best of things. He's got to, now,' replied Elf. 'Hey, where's Rebecca going?'

As the lorry roared and lurched along the main drive, Rebecca edged forward towards the driving cab, up front, hanging on to her white cap.

'Steady!' said Mike, catching her arm as she stumbled in her clogs. He smiled. 'You'll be the flying Dutchwoman if you're not careful!'

Rebecca reached the driving cabin, hung on tightly and peered round the side of it so that she could see the road ahead. Her lips parted in sudden excitement as she saw a flicker of white amongst the trees.

'Curly!'

She turned quickly and gave the thumbs-up sign. He stopped drumming, left the bandstand and came with uneven steps to the driver's cab. Then he started hammering loudly on the back of it.

'Mr Slade!' he shouted.

They were just passing the hidden figure.

'What is it, Watson?' yelled the housemaster, craning his neck out of the window and looking back at Curly. 'Want me to stop?'

'Just for a minute, sir!' Curly shouted. 'We're a girl

short. She had a bit of trouble with her costume! She's back there!'

The brakes screeched and the lorry juddered to a halt. The band played on loudly as a veiled figure in white raced out from behind a tree and ran to the back of the float. Mike bent over and lifted her aboard, swiftly.

'Okay, sir!' yelled Curly. 'We've got her!'

'Right-o!' The master revved up the engine and the lorry moved forward. He didn't even look back. 'That the lot? Let's get going.'

Mike held the girl steady and Curly weaved past the ticket office, almost tripping over the other girls' spreadeagled legs, to hug her exuberantly. Her half veil began to slip down from her face.

'Mara!' shrieked Tish, the first to recognize her.

'I made it!' Mara was laughing with joy. 'I made it!'

'Quick!' said Curly. He and Mike started to propel Mara along the moving float. 'Open the door, Tish – quick, Mara, get inside!'

Tish, Margot and Elf had all scrambled to their feet and they tugged the door of the ticket office open. As the boys pushed Mara inside the girls slapped her on the back, their dumbfounded surprise now giving way to delight.

'Mara – you had us completely fooled!'

'You weren't sick at all!'

'Oh, Mara – this is fantastic!'

'Ssssh!' Seated inside the dark ticket booth, Mara adjusted her veil and wagged a finger up at them as they shut the door and crowded round the hatch. Her large luminous brown eyes were full of amusement. 'I am not

Mara! I am a mysterious lady from Arabia and you have never seen me before in your lives!'

'Look at her!' said Curly in delight. 'Doesn't she look marvellous in there? Fascinating...mysterious...'

'A riddle wrapped in an enigma!' butted in Mike. 'Queen Cleopatra herself!'

'And I bet she'll sell loads of tickets!' added Curly. He turned to Rebecca, who had now joined them, hat askew and blue eyes watering with relief. 'Rebecca, that Arabian costume is out of this world! It's every bit as marvellous as Mara told me on the phone – nobody will know who it is! Nobody!'

They were turning out of the main gates.

'Come on, Curly – back on the drums!' shouted John Bates. 'We're about to make our first public appearance.'

'Rebecca!' said Tish. As the lorry turned out into the public highway, the four girls draped themselves around the box office into a pre-arranged tableau 'Oh, *Rebecca*!'

They looked at each other and laughed.

'How could you?' asked Tish.

'Yes, fancy keeping it secret from us!' said Margot.

'You rotten thing,' added Elf.

'I had to,' laughed Rebecca. 'It was hard enough with just *me* knowing!'

'She mustn't get found out!' declared Tish. It was exciting – it added spice to the day – but it was nerve-racking, too! 'We have to make sure of that! Even if I have to nip back to Crockers and get into that sick bed myself! Hey, Mara – '

'Ssssh!' said the veiled lips as the brown eyes peered out of the hatch.

'Sorry, I mean – er – Cleopatra. How did you leave things fixed with Matron?'

'I told her I just wanted to sleep and sleep!' hissed Mara. 'She gave me some tablets and I pretended to take them and then she tucked me up and left me some glucose drink in case I woke up. She said she'd wake me up at one o'clock to take my temperature again.'

'You've got all morning then!' said Rebecca in relief. 'When we break for lunch you can grab a taxi and get back to school!'

Margot and Elf, who'd been listening to all this rather anxiously, felt reassured.

People straggling into the town came in sight and Mara drew back so that she was completely out of sight. Rebecca glanced at Elf and Margot.

'Cheer up, you two,' she said confidently. 'Nothing will go wrong. Besides, it's done now!'

Rebecca wasn't going to admit to anyone how scared she'd been feeling. That she'd made this pact with Mara on the spur of the moment and ever since, in odd moments when she'd had time to think about it, she'd regretted it. But it was too late to think about that now!

As they drove slowly into the town, the boys began to play at full pitch – exciting, swinging music. Shoppers on the pavements stopped, cheering and waving as the float went past. A wintry sun came out from behind cloud and suddenly the girls started laughing with the sheer excitement of it all.

'Rebecca, you and Mara are fantastic, working all this out!' exclaimed Tish. 'It's the most brilliant idea I've ever come across.'

'Something we can tell our children about.' said Margot solemnly.

'Not to mention our grandchildren!' giggled Elf.

'I wonder how many tickets we'll sell?' wondered Rebecca.

They paraded once round the town, slowly, and the excitement grew. Children ran along after the float and three boys from Trebizon Tech drove behind them in an old yellow salloon car, banging the horn from time to time and waving scarves out of the car windows, which added to the general noise and fun. Finally Mr Slade parked the huge float in a corner of the market square, at the bottom end of the High Street, as had been arranged with the local police. A crowd surged round immediately.

By half past eleven the town's allocation of tickets was sold out! The remainder had to be kept back for the afternoon, for the villages.

The girls had brought a pile of school capes with them. As soon as all the tickets were sold they flung them over their costumes, for they were blue with cold and their teeth were chattering. John Slade had gone across to the Market Restaurant earlier. When he came back he found them standing by the float and running up and down on the spot to keep warm.

'The girls are freezing, sir!' said Curly. We'd better get them inside somewhere!'

'It's all fixed up,' nodded Mr Slade. He pointed above the restaurant to a big plate glass window on the first floor. 'I've booked the Market's upstairs room and hot lunch for the lot of you. You might as well get straight over there. I'll take the money back to school, Watson – '

As Curly handed over a locked attaché case, the master felt the weight of it and smiled broadly. He gave Curly a pat on the back.

'First rate idea of yours, Watson.' He beamed at Mara, who looked distinctly odd in a blue Trebizon cape and a white yashmak. 'First rate little ticket seller, too – everybody's been calling her Cleopatra!' He gazed round at all of them, approvingly. 'Well done, the lot of you. Take your time over lunch and get warm again. I'll be back in an hour and then we can start on the villages!'

He strode off and climbed into a waiting taxi with the case full of money, gave them a cheery wave and then departed.

'Yippee! Let's go and eat!' cried Tish.

Mara looked radiant. It had been a marvellous morning! Curly's idea was a success and she'd been able to help! Now Mr Slade was going to treat them to a hot meal!

But the sight of that taxi reminded her –

Her face fell.

'Maybe – maybe I ought to get back now – '

They all roared at her, furiously.

'Miss the food?' exclaimed the boys.

'Come on, Mara!' said Tish. 'You're safe for at least another hour!'

They surrounded her and lifted her up. She giggled helplessly as they carried her bodily across to the Market Restaurant chanting:

'Long live Queen Cleopatra!'

Lucy Hubbard parked her bike by the back door of Crockers. Stealthily she took a book out of the saddlebag, then gently eased the metal doors open and tip-toed into a long white-painted corridor that smelt faintly of disinfectant. A Second Year girl appeared in pyjamas and dressing-gown.

'Which room is Mara Leonodis in?' whispered Lucy. Nicola Hodges stared at her.

'Over there. Number 8. I saw Matron put her in there this morning. Hey – does anyone know you're here?'

'I'm only going to slip this book into the room for her to read!' hissed Lucy. 'Don't tell on me!'

'If you catch 'flu that's your look out,' said Nicola, with a shrug, going back into her own room. She had other things to think about. How was she going to win the Hilary Camberwell Music Scholarship when Matron wouldn't let her practise her violin?

Lucy tip-toed across to Mara's room, full of suppressed excitement. Nobody was interested in her theory, not even her mother. Especially her mother. 'You've come to Trebizon to work, not to waste time looking for grottos!' she'd told her daughter an hour ago. 'Now take your set book to the library and learn it off by heart. How could you bear to let Rebecca Mason beat you in the English test this week?'

'Mummy would have a fit if she could see me now!' thought Lucy. Just lately she'd been beginning to wonder about having her mother at Trebizon. It was a nuisance sometimes. 'But I know I won't catch 'flu! I'm sure Mara hasn't got a real illness. She's just unhappy that's all. She needs something really interesting to take

103

her mind off those silly boys. It's not really that much fun, dressing up and going on their freezing old lorry!'

Lucy looked at the book in her hand. She hoped that Mara would find it as exciting as she did. It wasn't her English set book. It was a rather dusty volume on local history that she'd found on a junk stall in the town on Wednesday afternoon. She eased open the door, gently.

'Mara!' she whispered.

Mara was under the blankets – she seemed to have pulled them right up over her head. Was she fast asleep? There was a glucose drink on her bedside locker, untouched. Oh, poor thing!

Lucy crossed the room and gently pulled the covers back.

'Mara – oh!'

She stared in shock. There was nobody there! Just a pillow and a rolled up school cape for the body and a bag stuffed full of night clothes for the head. She flung the covers back on top of them again and gazed wildly round the room. Mara had gone! She'd played a disgusting trick on everyone and gone down town! On that float.

Lucy didn't even stop to tell Matron. That would be too complicated because she'd get into trouble for being there! The main thing was to make sure that Mara was rescued – quickly – before anything happened to her. She rushed outside and put her book back in the saddlebag and then mounted her bike.

'She ought to be punished properly this time!' thought

Lucy, angrily. 'If she's been kidnapped it just serves her right! It'll teach her a lesson. I'll go straight and tell Mr Papaconstantopoulos what she's done!'

She pedalled her hardest along the main drive until she reached the school gates. Then she turned right towards the Trebizon Bay Hotel.

9
Mara Goes Missing

The meal had been delicious, a meal to remember. They'd had fresh local fish fried in golden brown batter with heaps of crinkly chips, followed by Chef's Gateau and lashings of hot coffee. The boys had gone back down to the float, but the girls were lingering over their coffee, laughing and talking excitedly and enjoying the panoramic view of the crowded market square with Trebizon High Street beyond, winding up hill towards the distant hotels.

But then Curly came rushing back.

'There's no need to get a taxi, Mara!' he said excitedly. 'Mr Slade wants to do the villages to the east first, so we'll go right by your school gates. I'll get him to drop you off there – you can be back in bed, ten minutes from now!'

'Great!' laughed Mara. 'I suppose you want that loan back – '

'No, no!' Curly spoke urgently. 'Don't bother now. Sir's sitting in the driving cab, waiting to go. Hurry up and drink that coffee.'

Both Tish and Mara had just poured themselves more coffee from the big pot. The others had finished.

'You three go on!' said Tish. 'Mara and I'll be down in two ticks!'

Rebecca, Margot and Elf rushed down the stairs after Curly.

'Better hurry up, Mara,' said Tish, swallowing down the last of her coffee. 'Mmmm. Delicious. Hey! What's the matter with you?'

Mara was staring out of the window, towards the top end of the High Street. There were people everywhere, but she had spotted two figures that she distinctly recognized. One was small and was holding a bicycle. The other was big and was talking to a policeman, who

108

was pointing this way, towards the big float parked in the market square.

'I don't believe it!' said Mara. Her face was white with anger. 'Oh, Tish, it can't be true!'

Down in the market square, Rebecca had to fight her way back on to the float. There was a lot of noise and confusion. A crowd of children had climbed aboard while they'd been having lunch and the boys were laughing and chasing them off. More shoppers had arrived and were clamouring for tickets and Mr Slade was leaning out of the driver's cab, trying to explain that they were sold out. The boys from Trebizon Tech were back and one of them was sitting on the bonnet of the yellow car, strumming a guitar.

Laughing with excitement, Rebecca straightened up the big banner Mara had made as Mr Slade sounded the horn loudly to signal that they were about to move off. Moments later, she caught a glimpse of her scrambling back on to the float in white veil and school cape, ducking into the ticket office – where was Tish? she must have got on the other side – and then the engine roared and the lorry started to move away. There were cheers and shouts.

The big vehicle crawled up the steep High Street and then, with a sudden juddering of brakes, it ground to a halt. A policeman was waving them down!

Rebecca, Margot and Elf stared at each other in horror.

The policeman was coming round to the back of the float accompanied by a great hulking figure in a purple sweater with a completely bald head.

'It's Papa!' gasped Rebecca.

Quite a crowd was gathering.

Curly's face had gone a sickly hue and the drum sticks dangled limply in his hands as the policeman called up to them.

'Now, I gather there's a young lady on here what shouldn't be here. Likely as not the one who's been wearing the veil all morning.'

He nodded to the big Greek, who immediately heaved himself on to the float. Papa looked at every face in turn and then strode straight over to the ticket office, opened the door, and pulled the occupant out. She was still wearing the blue cape and a pair of dark brown eyes gazed steadfastly at Papa above the mysterious half-veil.

They all waited and Rebecca felt her legs turn to jelly as slowly, very slowly, Papa took the veil away from the face.

Its owner was grinning broadly.

Tish!

Rebecca's whole body began to tremble with relief. She looked across to Curly and saw his eyes alight with joy. Papa was backing away, covered in confusion and embarrassment. He took one last, baffled look at each of the float's occupants in turn and then dropped off, over the side.

'False alarm?' asked the policeman, slightly irritable. A traffic jam was building up. He signalled to Mr Slade who was hanging out of the cab, looking impatient. 'Okay, sir! Full speed ahead. Sorry you've been troubled.'

The lorry roared away up the hill and Margot suddenly clutched Rebecca's arm.

'Look!'

Papa was talking to somebody in a shop doorway: a diminutive figure holding a bicycle. He appeared to be scolding her. It was Lucy Hubbard.

'Tish!' gasped Rebecca, as they helped her back into the ticket office. 'Lucy's back there – with Papa. How did you and Mara know – ?'

Tish was shaking with laughter.

'Mara spotted them! Was she furious – I've never seen anyone so furious in my life! She just gave me the headgear and fled!'

'D'you think she's found a taxi?' said Elf, weak with relief and excitement. 'D'you think she'll get back to school in time?'

'Surely!' exclaimed Tish. 'I don't know how Lucy suspected, but she looks a real fool now. She'll look an even bigger fool when they find Mara tucked safely up in bed at Crockers!'

They drove out of town and past Trebizon Bay, humming and swaying to the music of the band. What a morning! Mara would be in a taxi now, speeding back to school. With just the merest touch of luck, she should be safe! Lucy could suspect what she liked, but she couldn't prove a thing. They'd find Mara where she was supposed to be, fast asleep in bed at Crockers!

Only it didn't turn out like that at all.

'I'm surprised at you, Rebecca,' said Mrs Barrington. 'It was quite the worst turn you could have done for Mara,

111

encouraging her to go on the float. I've spent half the afternoon calming Mr Papaconstantopoulos down. He's convinced she's been kidnapped, but of course we know that's ridiculous.'

The four friends sat in Mrs Barrington's sitting room, still wearing their dressing-up clothes. The ticket-selling in the villages had been a great success and they'd arrived back at Court House with half an hour to spare before tea. But before they'd even had time to change, they'd been hauled in to see the house mistress. Mrs Barrington was feeling very irritated with them.

'I'm sorry,' said Rebecca, the picture of misery.

Mara hadn't come back to her sick bed, after all. Lucy Hubbard had reported everything to Mrs Barrington as soon as she'd arrived back at Court House and put her cycle away. Mrs Barrington had at once phoned Matron who had, in fact, been right on the point of phoning *her* . . . having just that minute discovered that what she'd taken to be the sleeping figure of Mara all morning was no more than some things piled under the blankets!

After that, prefects had hunted everywhere for Mara, but she was nowhere to be found.

'You'd better get changed and then go and have tea,' Mrs Barrington said wearily. 'It's obvious that Mara is in a fine old sulk because her bodyguard came hunting for her, just when she was having a good time. I expect she's hiding somewhere. However, it's a cold day and a little hunger can work wonders. Let's hope she turns up when she hears the tea-bell go.'

The friends went through to the main part of the boarding house silent and woebegone. Their costumes

112

looked bedraggled and the worse for wear and they were cold and hungry. They'd had their fun – marvellous fun – and now they were going to pay for it. So was Mara! They just couldn't bear to think what her father's reaction would be when he heard about all this.

As they trailed into their rooms, Lucy Hubbard peeped across the corridor, hardly able to conceal her satisfaction.

'They don't think it's so funny now!' she told Anne Finch. 'I bet you anything you like that Mara's been kidnapped!'

'Oh, do be quiet,' said Anne. 'Anybody would think you wanted her to be, the way you've been carrying on.'

'She's just hiding somewhere,' said Ann Ferguson. 'Probably wants to teach her father a lesson. That's just what I'd do!'

While Tish and Rebecca were changing, Sue arrived back from Garth College and they told her everything. She was horrified.

'I *wondered* why Papa couldn't bring me back from rehearsals! I was told to catch the minibus, because he was busy somewhere. Busy looking for Mara as it turns out! Oh, *crikey!*'

They lost no time in setting off for the dining hall. Elf and Margot raced on ahead, hoping against hope they would see Mara there. The other three took their time, keeping their eyes open all the way for some sign of her. It was getting dark now.

'D'you think she *will* turn up for tea?' asked Rebecca, as they passed the little lake in front of the music school. 'Can Mrs Barry be right and she's just in a temper?'

'She was in a temper all right,' said Tish, frowning. 'But I took it for granted that she'd just rush back to that sick room as fast as possible.'

'If only she had!' exclaimed Sue, in despair. 'She might still have got away with it! If Matron had found her asleep in bed when Lucy came back telling tales to Mrs Barry, I bet Mrs Barry would have told Lucy a thing or two!'

'Yes,' said Rebecca thoughtfully, 'Mrs B. might have given Mara a terrific lecture afterwards, but somehow I don't think it would have gone any farther. Oh, why did Mara have to go and do something stupid!'

'Let's hope it's nothing too stupid,' said Tish uneasily.

At any rate, Mara didn't turn up for tea.

'Rebecca – here a minute.'

Straight after tea, Rebecca had rushed to the sports centre. She was beginning to feel slightly panicky about Mara and more than a little responsible too. She'd had the wild idea that Mara might be hiding at the sports centre and she'd searched all the shower cubicles. What a waste of time!

She was just on the point of leaving through the glass doors when she was stopped by Miss Willis and Joss Vining.

'Josselyn wants to tell you her news, Rebecca,' said the games mistress. 'I think you know something about it, already.'

One look at their portentous faces was enough for Rebecca. The thing that she'd been pushing out of her mind since Wednesday now came flooding back to her.

'It's true then?' she said to Joss. 'You're going?'

'Just for a year,' said Joss. 'I'm going to the States.'

A whole year, thought Rebecca. *The year I really need you.*

'Joss's father's going to be working in California for a year. There's a marvellous coaching set-up there and so Joss is going with him. All the officials here agree that it's absolutely the right thing for her at this stage in her game.'

'It sounds marvellous,' said Rebecca, trying to hide her woe. 'I – I'll miss you, Joss.'

'What you need now, Rebecca, is to enter some competitions in the Easter holidays,' said Miss Willis. She looked worried. 'I gather it's rather difficult with your parents abroad . . .'

'Yes,' said Rebecca. She and Mrs Ericson had been talking about it then! 'I don't see how I can.'

'If only you were that bit further on, we might have been able to get a sponsorship for you,' said Miss Willis. 'If you'd done well in some tournaments by now a local business might have been interested . . . but, of course, you've hardly had time yet. It's no use our thinking about that.'

Rebecca wanted to get away. She couldn't bear all this, not just now! Sara Willis could sense it.

'Run along and don't look so worried. This is a setback for you, but it's not the end of the world. We'll give you all the support we can at Trebizon, with or without Joss. We'll try and find you the competition you need in term time, even if we can't help in the holidays. Off you go!

Gratefully, Rebecca pushed open the swing doors and ran outside. She heard Joss call out:

'Hey, Rebecca, is it true that Mara's gone missing?'

'Yes!' Rebecca flung back at her, running along the paved footpath, through pools of lamplight, away from the centre. Then the glass doors swung shut, leaving Joss in the warm and Rebecca out in the cold. *If you hadn't dropped your bombshell, Joss, I'd never have been in that silly mood in the first place*! thought Rebecca angrily. *I'd never have let Mara go on the float.* But even as that thought crossed her mind, she dismissed it. She was being unfair! She was just making excuses for herself!

She got back to Court House in time to see Papa drawing away in the big black car. He looked dispirited. Mrs Barrington was standing beneath the porch light with the other four, watching him go. Obviously, Mara still hadn't shown up. Rebecca walked across and joined them.

'Papa's just been back to check,' said Tish helplessly. 'Now he's going to look round the town for about the tenth time. And he's got my photo of Mara and he's going to show it to all the cab drivers.'

'I've phoned Syon House and asked Mr Slade to question his boys,' said Mrs Barrington briskly. If she were beginning to get worried she wasn't going to show it. 'This could be some silly publicity stunt for the concert.'

'She paused. Then went on briskly, 'You five go and put your heads together. You know Mara best – where she could be hiding. Oh, and I've spoken to Miss Welbeck. If Mara hasn't shown up by eight o'clock she feels she'll have to inform the police.'

116

10
Trying to Solve the Mystery

Back in Court House, girls appeared in the hall and on the stairs, asking questions. But the five friends brushed them all aside and made directly for the nearer of their two rooms.

'Sorry, Jenny, we just want to be quiet a while,' said Tish, meeting her at the door. 'We've got to try and *think*.'

'Let Jane and me make you some coffee or something then,' said Jenny Brook-Hayes. 'Where do you think Mara can have *got* to?'

'That's just what we want to think about!' said Rebecca irritably. 'Oh, sorry, Jen. No, don't bother about coffee.'

They went inside and shut the door and Rebecca sat down on her bed and buried her face in her hands.

'If anything's happened to Mara, it's all my fault. I should never have let her try on that blasted costume in the first place – '

'Stop it, Becky,' said Tish. 'We've got to find her, that's all.'

'We've *got* to think where she is!' agreed Sue. 'I can't believe anything's happened to her – but if it gets so that the police are called in, the whole thing will blow up and be in the papers and Mara's father – '

She didn't go on. She didn't have to. But Elf burst into tears.

'He'd just take her away from Trebizon straight away.'

'If it's anybody's fault, it's Lucy Hubbard's,' said Margot in a cold fury.

'Look you lot, we can do without the post mortems,' said Tish. She was walking up and down the small room, banging her right fist into her left palm. Her voice was steady. 'We've solved mysteries before, haven't we –

118

Action Committee, remember? Let's try and solve this one. Let's go through all the possibilities for a start – '

Tish was a steadying influence at times like this. They all started to think properly about it.

'Well, number one, there's what Mrs Barry was suggesting,' said Rebecca. 'A publicity stunt. Curly laughed about it once. Kidnapping Mara from the float – remember?'

'But Curly would never – '

'Of course not,' agreed Rebecca. 'But some other crackbrained boys at Garth could have got to hear that Mara was on the float this morning and might have grabbed her before she could get back to school. Just to raise more money for the Children's Fund...'

'It's possible,' said Sue, slowly. 'But surely a ransom note would have appeared by now. So everybody would know it was strictly for laughs.'

'If that's what's happened, they'll find Mara any minute now!' said Elf, cheering up briefly. 'Mr Slade's questioning all the boys. Mrs Barry's asked him to! Once they know how serious it is...'

'I don't think that *is* what's happened,' said Tish flatly. 'As Sue says, no ransom note. Besides, Mara would have raised the roof and made them let her go.'

'But you said she was in a fury, Tish. Maybe she *liked* being kidnapped,' Rebecca pointed out.

'Ah, that brings me to my theory, theory number two,' said Tish.

'What's that?' they asked eagerly.

'Well, just the simple, obvious one. Mara wants to teach her father a lesson. She wants to give him the fright of his life. So either she *is* hiding, somewhere really clever where we'll never find her. Or else – '

'She's run away?' realised Sue. 'She threatened to do that, remember? The day after the disco – the day we all had to go and see Miss Welbeck!'

Talk of the disco reminded Rebecca of something.

'My bike!' she said. She jumped up, took her torch from the top of her chest of drawers and ran and opened the sash window. 'I'll go to the cycle shed. Wait here. Let's see if Mara's taken a bike, mine in particular. She likes it.'

She went out by way of the window and returned three minutes later. Margot helped her back in.

'Well?'

Rebecca shook her head.

'No. All the bikes are there. If she has run away, she's gone on foot.'

'What about train?' asked Sue. 'Or hitching a lift?'

'In a long white Arabian gown?' queried Tish. 'That's all she was wearing when she did a bunk out of the back door of the Market Restaurant. I put a cape over my highland gear to pretend I was her – remember? But she didn't even bother with a cape. Come to think of it, we left the other one behind in the restaurant.'

'Is that all she's wearing, that dress?' said Rebecca. 'You never told us that, Tish.'

'I've only just thought about it. Wherever she is, she must be freezing by now. Though I suppose she's got a jumper underneath.'

'She has,' said Rebecca. 'But if she's still wearing that dress, then she can't have run away! She might have been in a rage, but she's not that silly! She'd know full

120

well that she wouldn't get far dressed like that. Somebody would be bound to stop her and ask questions.'

'Probably,' nodded Tish. She sighed. 'That brings us back where we started. The only thing that makes sense is Mara's hiding. And I don't think there'd be anywhere in the town. She'd want somewhere safe and warm and completely concealed – '

'Somewhere in the school, or the school grounds!' said Margot. 'Some place she knows well.'

'The prefects have been looking all afternoon,' said Elf.

'Well, I think we'd better look again,' retorted Tish. 'Let's get our capes and torches and get going.' She looked at her watch. 'Less than an hour to go now – ten past seven.'

They must find Mara before the police were called in!

They went out by way of the window; they didn't want half the girls in Court House following them. They wanted to think carefully – what sort of place might Mara choose to hide in?

'What about the basement in old school?' suggested Sue.

They crossed the courtyard and skirted round Norris House, then cut across the hockey pitches to get to main school quickly, their torch beams bobbing ahead of them. There was no moon.

Somebody was following them, but they didn't notice.

On the other side of the hockey pitches they cut into the dense shrubbery that sheltered old school from the east. The leaves rustled and whispered as they brushed through them and sometimes sudden shadows made them jump. They emerged from the bushes and stood above stone steps that led down to a basement door in old building.

'We haven't even considered theory number three,' Elf said suddenly. Her voice was little more than a whisper. 'That – that someone really has kidnapped Mara.'

They all looked at her uneasily.

She looked sheepish.

'I know it sounds silly, but when we went through those bushes just then, I suddenly thought of that funny little man I saw in the churchyard. The one in the pin-striped suit. I – I think he really could have been hiding.'

'Elf!' gasped Rebecca.

A cold shiver ran down her spine as a piece of a jig-saw fell into place in her mind. She remembered the man she'd seen sitting in staff gardens on Wednesday – just after Joss had dropped her bombshell.

'What is it, Rebeck?' rapped Sue.

'Small? Pin-striped suit? Rimless glasses?' asked Rebecca.

Elf nodded, uneasily.

'I've seen him, too!' Rebecca exclaimed.

'When?' clamoured the others. 'Where?'

She told them, hesitantly.

'I was in a blur at the time but there seemed something familiar about him. I just couldn't put my finger on it. Now I realise why – I'd never seen him before in my life. But I had a *mental* picture of him from the time you told us about him, Elf.'

'So it couldn't have been a day girl's father who'd come to church, then?' said Margot, worriedly. 'I mean one of those Dads would hardly be hanging round the school in the middle of the week. Who was he, then?'

'The window cleaner I expect!' said Tish impatiently. 'For heaven's sake let's stop being morbid. He probably had a perfectly good reason for being here both times. We know Mara's only hiding. Let's get a move on and try and find her.'

Tish was steadying them again. They descended the steps to the basement door, suddenly feeling reassured.

Except Rebecca.

There had been something about that man. She could see him clearly now, a vivid flashback flung up suddenly from the dark recesses of her mind. Something purposeful. He had been waiting – and watching. But for what?

They emerged up the steps half an hour later, tired and dispirited. It had been a formidable job searching the basement.

It ramified in all directions under old school and they had searched every corner, cupboard and corridor.

'Now what?' asked Rebecca, brushing the cobwebs off her cape.

They all stood there in a huddle at the top of the stone steps, feeling helpless. Suddenly they heard running footsteps.

'Hey!'

A small figure in an oversize cape came flapping round the corner of the big building, waving an arm. As she drew near, Rebecca flashed her torch over her.

'Lucy Hubbard!'

'What do *you* want?' asked Tish furiously.

Lucy came straight up to them, slightly out of breath, trembling a little with excitement.

'I want to speak to you.'

'Well we don't want to speak to *you*,' said Sue. 'Have you no idea how worried we are about Mara and it's all your fault! You've got a nerve showing your face near us.'

'I'm the one who's been worried about Mara all along!' said Lucy self-righteously. 'I *knew* she'd be kidnapped one day and all she's ever done is laugh about it. She's had her lesson now!'

Rebecca grabbed Lucy and shook her angrily. She was so tense she was at snapping point.

'Shut up! Shut up! If you hadn't shown up in town this morning none of this would have happened. Mara was only having some fun. How would you like to be hemmed in all the time, the way she's been all term? How would you like to have a watchdog following you around? Never feeling free!'

Lucy went suddenly very quiet and pale, not from the physical shaking but from the intensity of Rebecca's emotion. She was staring at her as though she almost understood for the first time – as though Rebecca's words had come as something of a revelation.

'All right, then.' Rebecca let go of Lucy. Her hands dropped to her side. 'What do you want?' she asked wearily. 'What did you want to speak to us about?'

'I – I – ' Lucy's lips had gone dry and she licked them. The others were watching her with interest, now.

'What were you going to say?' prompted Tish.

'It's just – well, it's nothing really,' began Lucy. 'It's only that when I cycled back from the town at lunch time I came Churchgate way and I saw a car parked outside Churchgate. There was nobody in it. I don't suppose it means a thing – '

'What are you suggesting then?' asked Sue.

'Well,' Lucy said, feebly. She was still looking subdued. 'I suppose if somebody did kidnap Mara, they could have brought her in that car and locked her up – well, in the church, or somewhere like that.'

'It's certainly a funny place to park a car,' mused Rebecca.

They all looked at each other. Churchgate was a minor entrance to the Trebizon grounds, on the far distant side from the main gates. It was approached by a narrow winding lane that came directly up from the town and led nowhere in particular. Day girls parents used the lane to drive up to church on Sundays. Trebizon's own little church, St Mary's, lay just inside the gate. But otherwise cars never came up the lane as there were no farms or houses along it, just one or two cottages back towards the town. Why had a car been parked there at lunch time?

'We might as well go and have a look,' said Tish.

Lucy stood and stared before deciding to walk slowly back to Court House. The friends turned their backs on her and ran as fast as they could across the grass, five bobbing lights and silhouettes, until St Mary's Church came in sight.

11

Tish is Proved Right – Or is She?

Rebecca was the fastest runner and she reached the wicket gate first. It gave a long, low creak as she pushed it open. There was still no moon and the church looked eerie, a dark mass huddled amongst the trees. Bare branches moaned and swayed in the winter wind.

They five of them walked in nervous procession up the path, through the churchyard. Elf glanced nervously at the granite tombstone where the man had been concealed and hurried past it, as though fearful he might jump out. They reached the oak door into the porch and pushed it open.

'Find the light switches,' said Sue. 'It's too creepy here for my liking.'

Rebecca walked into the church with her torch beam cast ahead of her. She tiptoed past the silent pews and the little marble font, where the babies of the manor house had once been christened, then through thick velvet curtains that swished behind her, into the vestry. She tripped over a dustpan and brush in the darkness and the loud clatter made the others, out there in the aisle, jump with fright.

Shivering a little and hardly daring to look at the darkness all around her, Rebecca moved her torch beam along the wall until she found the main light switch. She plunged it on and the church flooded with electric light. The others came rushing in to join her.

They all blinked in the light and looked around them. Tish was the first one to reach the door to the bell tower.

'It's bolted!' she exclaimed. 'She could be up here!'

They slid the bolts back and Tish and Sue used their torches to find the way up the narrow, winding staircase to the tower, in single file. The others waited below, holding back their voices.

'Oh.' Rebecca exhaled in disappointment as Tish's echoing shout came down – *Nobody here* !

They heard the clatter of footsteps coming down the stone steps as Tish and Sue descended. They emerged in the vestry with their blue capes smudged with white dust, where they'd brushed against the thick stone walls of the tower.

'Nobody up there at all?' asked Elf, crestfallen.

'Only a few spiders and bats,' replied Tish. Margot shuddered.

'The crypt!' Rebecca said then. 'That's the other possibility.'

They stomped through the church, up towards the altar, and then turned left through a doorway just in front of the choir stalls which smelt strongly of wax polish. The flight of stairs leading down to the crypt was in darkness. This part of the church wasn't on the main lighting circuit. Rebecca, leading the way, was about to click her torch back on, then stopped. She grabbed Tish's arm in excitement.

'Look!' she hissed. She pointed down to the stout wooden door of the crypt. It was firmly closed but a crack of light showed at the bottom.

'The light's on in the crypt!' whispered Tish. 'There must be somebody in there!'

The five of them almost fell down the last few steps in their haste and came up hard against the door. Sue turned the handle.

'That's funny,' she said. 'It won't open – '

Tish pulled Sue back and pointed to the ancient black iron key that was sitting firmly in its keyhole.

'It must be locked,' she said.

They all gathered round. They were too excited to be nervous now. Tish took a firm grip on the big key and slowly turned it back to unlock the door. It moved easily and silently in the lock with just the tiniest little 'click' to show that the door was now open.

They pushed the door open, inch by inch.

They could see a naked electric light bulb hanging from the ceiling, glowing brightly, lighting up the crypt. They pushed and shoved each other and crowded through the open doorway –

'Look!' cried Rebecca in excitement. 'Food!'

They rushed to an old oak settle, standing with its back against the thick, damp walls of the crypt. On the settle there was an empty cardboard provision box. Piled around it were empty crisp bags, two used drinks cans, three apple cores and a cardboard carton covered in pictures of miniature chocolate rolls.

'Salt and vinegar!' cried Elf, picking up one of the crisp bags. 'Mara's favourite sort!'

'And her favourite canned drink, too!' exclaimed Margot, pointing. 'Lemonade and lime. She's drunk two big cans of it!'

She was picking up the cake carton and examining it.

'She's a glutton for mini choc rolls, too. She seems to have eaten the whole box of them.'

Tish and Rebecca were looking all round the crypt. Tish was laughing. 'So she got a lift up from the town in that car Lucy Hubbard saw! Where is she now, though?'

They scouted round for a few moments, peering behind the huge stone pillars that supported the roof.

There was no sign of Mara. The crypt was empty.

'Never mind. It proves we're on the right track,' said Tish. She was elated in her relief. 'Mara just wanted to give Papa and everyone a big fright – the way she always threatened she would!'

'Where's she gone now?' wondered Sue, stuffing the remains of Mara's feast into the cardboard box and then putting it under her arm. 'She obviously got fed up with sitting down here for hours – ' She shivered and looked round at the damp walls. 'Can't say I blame her!'

'Gone to find somewhere warmer, I expect,' said Elf, joyfully.

'She might even be back at Court House by now.' Margot suggested. 'We could have missed her.'

'Hey!' said Tish, suddenly looking at her watch. 'Do you realise it's nearly eight o'clock? If Mara isn't back yet, we've got to stop Miss Welbeck calling in the police. Come on, quick! Bring the box, Sue, we can show Mrs Barry.'

Tish led the rush to the door. Elf brought up the rear and flipped the light off as she left the crypt.

'There's Papa to think about, too.' gasped Sue. 'We've got to let *him* know everything's okay, before he starts phoning Mara's father in Athens or something awful like that.'

They all raced away from the church, not even stopping to turn the main lights off. They could see to all that, later. Rebecca ran with them, but she kept looking back.

'What's the matter, Becky?' puffed Tish as they ran.

'Nothing!'

Rebecca didn't like to say anything, not just yet. But she thought it distinctly odd of Mara to leave all that mess in the crypt and the light still burning. Of course, it would make sense if she'd only intended to slip out for a very short time.

In which case, why bother to lock the door after her? It didn't quite add up, somehow.

The five girls were just heading across the forecourt towards the front door of Court House when they heard the sound of a horn behind them, the screech of brakes. They found themselves trapped in the headlights of the Barringtons' car, their long shadows pinioned to the wall. They turned as their house mistress called out to them, then hurried back and crowded round the car.

'Any sign?' she asked, winding the window fully down. 'I think I'd better let Miss Welbeck call the police now. It's five minutes to eight.'

She looked rather weary. Both she and her husband had been driving slowly, round and round the grounds, having a last look for Mara.

'No – don't! It's all right.' exclaimed Sue, holding up the cardboard box and smiling. 'Mara's perfectly safe – if she's not back by now, she should be pretty soon. She's run out of food – look!'

'We've found out where she's been hiding all afternoon' Elf explained. 'Down in the church crypt – I should think she's caught pneumonia!'

'Oh, the silly girl,' said Mrs Barrington, climbing out of the car. She looked very relieved. 'Let's go inside in the warm and have a look at that box you're holding,

132

Sue.' She bent and called through the car window. 'It's all right darling, I think you can put the car away.'

Rebecca and Tish were already running on ahead to the boarding house.

'Let's see if she's come back!' said Tish.

As they burst in through the front door they almost collided with Lucy Hubbard.

'Did you find her?' Lucy asked eagerly.

'Almost,' said Tish. 'You did something sensible at last, telling us about that car you saw at lunch time.'

'Isn't she back here yet?' Rebecca rapped to Lucy.

'No.' Lucy was startled. 'Didn't you find her, then? What do you mean, almost?' she asked Tish. 'I mean, either you found her or you didn't find her.'

At that moment Mrs Barrington came in with the others and put the box on the hall table running her fingers through the rubbish inside.

Girls were hanging over the stairs, listening.

'Now, tell me about it quickly, you lot. Miss Welbeck will be phoning through at any moment, to see whether she should call the police or not. You're sure these crisp bags and things are Mara's – ?'

'Positive!' said Elf.

'Oh, look – here's Papa back!' exclaimed Sue, as she saw the shape of the big black car drawing up outside the front porch. 'We can tell him to stop worrying now.'

Quickly she explained to Mrs Barrington why they knew that the food had been Mara's and the house mistress nodded.

'I think we can take it that Mara's very near to home,' she said with a smile. 'As you say, she probably got cold

133

and miserable in the crypt and has found somewhere warmer. She must be getting very, very bored by now. I'm sure it won't be long before – ' She glanced at her watch. 'I won't wait for Miss Welbeck to phone, I'll ring her myself. I'll go by the front way and have a very quick word with Mr Papaconstantopoulos first.'

The girls stood back to let her through. She took two steps towards the front door when suddenly a shrill voice rang out.

'Mrs Barrington! Don't go. Please – wait a minute – '

They all looked round in astonishment. Lucy Hubbard stood rigidly in the common room doorway. She was pale and trembly. There were tears in her eyes.

'Whatever's the matter, Lucy?' asked the house mistress, frowning. She came back up the hall. The girls stepped aside again and watched as she walked up to Lucy and took her by the arm. 'What's wrong?'

'I – I've been listening to everything!' said Lucy. 'And now I know. Mara isn't safe at all. She really *has* been kidnapped – she must have been!'

12
A Matter of Life and Death

'What do you mean, you stupid girl?' asked Mrs
Barrington irritably. 'Who on earth would want to

kidnap Mara? I think we can be fairly certain that she's safely in school bounds somewhere – '

'No!' screamed Lucy. 'Somebody's taken her from the church crypt! They must have done!'

There was a lot of whispering and scuffling overhead as more girls crushed down on to the staircase, pushing each other to get a good view over the banisters. Mrs Barrington looked up sharply.

'Scoot – all of you! Go on. Up to your rooms!'

Then the house mistress led Lucy towards the kitchen, nodding to Rebecca & Co. to follow.

'Calm down, Lucy, for goodness' sake. I think we'd better have a talk.'

As she opened the kitchen door, Jane Bowen, Jenny Brook-Hayes and Anne Finch fell out, having been listening hard. '*Scoot!*' said Mrs Barrington and they quickly fled to their rooms.

'Now, sit down, Lucy, and try and explain to us what you're talking about.'

They were alone in the kitchen. The house mistress, the tiny newcomer to Court House and Mara's five friends. Rebecca and Tish stood with their backs pressed against the kitchen door, keeping it firmly closed.

'I saw Mara come back from town at lunch time!' Lucy blurted out. 'Some boys in a yellow car gave her a lift up to school. They stopped on the way back and went in a shop to buy food for her. And a torch, I believe. Then they came up the little lane, back to school Churchgate way. I kept them in sight all the time, racing on my bike.'

'The Trebizon Tech boys!' exclaimed Rebecca.

136

'Go on, Lucy,' said Mrs Barrington icily.

Lucy was so frightened by now that she could hardly get the words out fast enough.

'I concealed myself and watched them park the car! They let Mara out, with the box of food and cheered and honked the horn as she ran over to the church. They shouted things like: *Don't you let them find you, darling*! and *Good luck*! and then they drove off. It made me *sick*,' Lucy added vehemently.

'And you've kept all this to yourself!' said Mrs Barrington angrily. But she was baffled. 'I fail to see what all the melodrama's about, Lucy. Whatever makes you think that someone's taken Mara away from the crypt against her will?'

'Lucy hasn't finished yet,' said Rebecca, tersely.

'What happened next, Lucy?' asked Sue, catching on.

'I – I – ' Lucy hung her head, unable to speak.

'Let me guess,' said Rebecca. Her heart was banging hard. 'You thought it was about time that Mara was taught a lesson – and the rest of us, too. A lesson we'd never forget. After the boys had gone, you crept into the church after Mara, tip-toed down to the crypt and very quietly – '

'Turned the key!' ended Sue.

Lucy couldn't speak. She just nodded. There was a sickened silence.

Tish looked as though she were going to hit her.

'Mara hates being shut in anywhere!' she raged. 'You little fool. At first she wouldn't realise she was locked in that place – but once she did – '

'I never thought about how she'd be feeling,' sobbed

Lucy. 'I just wanted you all to realise how dangerous it was for Mara to disobey her father. I wanted you to be really scared, but you still wouldn't take it seriously, any of you. Not even Mrs Barry! So I just decided to wait until you got really upset and then *I'd* be the one to think of where she was and you'd all like me – '

'The heroine of the story!' said Sue, with bitter sarcasm.

'Never mind all this nonsense!' said Mrs Barrington. She was drumming her fingers on the windowsill, looking out into the darkness. 'I can see exactly why Lucy is so frightened. Mara couldn't have got out of the locked crypt *on her own*. She must have shouted and banged and somebody must have heard her. But who was it? Who released her? With half the school looking for her, why hasn't the person come forward?'

She pushed her way out of the kitchen. They trooped out behind her, white-faced. Papa was waiting stoically in the hall. His big, kindly face was crumpled up with worry. He was looking at Tish's snapshot of Mara, in his hand.

'We didn't want the police in, did we, Papa? But I think they have to be called in now. I'm sorry.'

He nodded.

'Come through to the house with me.' She took his arm. 'Help yourself to coffee while I 'phone the principal.'

About to disappear through her private door, she remembered Lucy. She turned and called out to her in a cold, furious voice:

'Go and sit in the common room and wait until I summon you. I'd like your mother to be here when we

138

talk about your behaviour today.'

As soon as Mrs Barrington had gone the hall filled with girls, thronging round, talking excitedly, asking questions. Tish and the others, very pale and shaken, had gathered round the coinbox phone under the stairs and were trying to get through to Syon House. Maybe Curly would know something! Maybe Mara had turned up there by now!

But Rebecca had gone.

She was running through the night, shining her torch, faster than she'd ever run before. Her fair hair streamed out behind her, her cape billowed, her eyes watered in the wind. When, at last, St Mary's Church came in sight, the lights were on as they'd left them and its three stained glass windows glowed out against the blackness.

In her private sitting room, Mrs Barrington had phoned Miss Welbeck first. The principal had at once contacted the police. Now the house mistress put through a call to staff quarters and asked to speak to Mrs Hubbard.

She was kept hanging on for a while. Then Miss Heath came to the phone and explained that Mrs Hubbard's husband had collected her at six thirty as apparently they'd arranged to dine together at a local restaurant. She should be back shortly. Was there any message?

Mrs Barrington said yes, it was urgent. Could Mrs Hubbard come across to Court House as soon as she returned? If she were able to bring her husband with her, so much the better. It concerned their daughter, Lucy.

Of course, it was the job of the police to find Mara.

139

Rebecca knew that. But she couldn't wait!

She didn't think for a moment that Mara could have gone to Garth College.

Mara was in some kind of terrible danger! Rebecca just knew she was! She'd never liked the idea of the crypt being left untidy, with the light still on. It simply wasn't like Mara to leave it like that – not of her own free will!

What had happened to her?

There was something else that puzzled Rebecca. If somebody had unlocked the door and taken Mara away from the crypt, why had they carefully locked the door again afterwards? It didn't make sense.

Supposing she'd never left the crypt! Supposing she were still in there!

'But where?' wondered Rebecca. '*Where?*'

She entered the silent church, panting. She walked unsteadily up the aisle towards the choir stalls, trying to get her breath back, then turned through the little doorway that led down to the crypt. She flashed her torch down the stone steps and saw at the bottom that the door of the crypt was ajar just as they'd left it. Her footsteps set up a chilling, sepulchral echo as she descended.

If only she'd stopped Mara going on the float in the first place, none of this would have happened! If anything had happened to Mara then in a way she, Rebecca Mason, was responsible.

The crypt was in darkness because they'd switched the light off when they'd fled from there earlier. Rebecca edged her way forward and opened the door a little wider. She stood in the doorway, running her torch beam over the near wall, searching for the light switch.

She couldn't find it.

She wanted to go in, but she didn't dare. The crypt smelt musty and damp. The cavernous darkness in front of her reminded her of a huge tomb. It had seemed all right before, when there'd been five of them! Now, on her own... Her legs started to turn to jelly. She suddenly remembered vague stories she'd heard about the crypt...a nobleman's daughter...untimely death...ghosts.

What had happened to Mara?

Torch trembling a little in her hand, she tried again to find the light switch. Then –

She heard a distant moaning sound!

Her scalp went prickly all over.

'Who – who's that?' she called. 'M-mara?'

Just her own voice came echoing back. At last she saw the light switch, edged towards it in the darkness and fumbled it on.

She looked round, blinking, in the light. The crypt was empty!

'M-mara?' she called again. 'Was – was that you?'

Shaking with fear she began to edge her way round the inside wall of the crypt, glancing behind each pillar as she passed it, calling over and over again. Still this terrible sense of danger for Mara. Still just the sound of her own voice echoing, followed by silence.

'I did hear something, I *did*,' Rebecca told herself. 'A moaning noise – where did it come from?'

She'd reached the far side of the crypt now. There was a memorial plaque set in the damp wall, the faded gold lettering half hidden under patches of mould. *In Loving Memorie of the Ladye Emily*... Rebecca shivered. She remembered now. Wasn't it the Ladye Emily who was supposed to haunt the crypt? The daughter of the nobleman who'd built Trebizon in the eighteenth century and the apple of his eye. She was supposed to have died tragically at the age of seventeen.

Suddenly the plaque appeared to move. Rebecca jumped back, staring at it. The light was very dim this side of the crypt – were her eyes playing tricks? There was something not quite right about the plaque: it seemed to sit unevenly in the stone wall.

Slowly, very slowly, Rebecca reached out a hand to touch it.

This time it really did move! It seemed to be on secret hinges!

Rebecca looked down to the floor – there were chunks of old mortar lying there. Somebody had pulled away the pieces of cracking mortar that held the plaque embedded in the wall and now –

She took hold of the free edge and pulled it towards her. It opened like a little door! There was nothing behind, just darkness. Rebecca flashed on her torch and shone the beam into the darkness.

'A secret tunnel!' she gasped. She began to shake. The dank, black hole confronted her menacingly but it wasn't ghosts she was frighened about any more, it was Mara. She cupped a hand to her mouth –

'Mara!'

Her voice echoed and re-echoed along the narrow tunnel, but no reply came. Quickly Rebecca shed her hampering cape and let it fall on the flagstoned floor. She hoisted herself up into the tunnel entrance and wriggled into it, glad of the thick jeans that protected her knees from the rough floor.

She edged along on all fours, the torch gripped in her teeth. The tunnel grew wider, turned a corner, then suddenly narrowed again. The air was stale and suffocating. She rested on her elbows and took the torch in her hand again.

'Mara!' she called.

She moved the beam in an arc and realised that the tunnel had caved in further on, leaving only a very narrow opening.

'Mara!' she called again, urgently. Her heart began to beat very fast. She crawled deeper into the tunnel until she reached the blockage.

She flashed her torch through the narrow gap – and screamed.

'Mara! Mara! Are you all right?'

Mara was lying a few feet beyond the gap, trapped by what must have been the sudden caving in of the next stretch of tunnel. She was lying on her side, hopelessly pinned down. It wasn't possible to see her face because loose earth and small stones had buried it. But Rebecca recognized the white gossamer gown, peeping here and there through the rubble.

'Mara!' whispered Rebecca. She must be suffocating! She must get to her, quickly, and get all that stuff cleared away from her face so that she could breathe properly –

If it weren't too late.

Rebecca tried to squeeze through the narrow gap, but

her shoulders stuck. She wriggled and squirmed and tried to get through from every angle, but she couldn't. She started clawing away at the rocks, trying to make the gap wider, but they wouldn't budge and her hands started to bleed.

'Mara!' Rebecca moaned.

There was only one thing to do. Get the police, firemen, ambulances...they'd clear the tunnel and get through to Mara! Only by then, surely, it would be too late? She backed down the tunnnel as fast as she could go, sobbing quietly, then lowered herself back into the crypt.

'Rebecca!'

Rebecca swung round, staring eyed.

Somebody was running towards her, carrying a torch. Lucy Hubbard!

'Mara's trapped in there – I can't get to her – she's suffocating – ' wept Rebecca. 'I can't get through, I'm too big – '

Lucy let her cape drop to the floor on top of Rebecca's and heaved herself up into the opening. Her face had gone very white, but she looked determined.

'I'm small!'

She disappeared into the tunnel. Rebecca climbed in behind her.

'Hold you torch in your mouth. I'm right behind you. Keep going!' she gasped. Then, after a while: 'Look, there's the gap, ahead of you. Can you get through? Please say you can get through!'

She caught up with her, by the gap. Lucy was peering through, flashing her torch. Then she turned and looked full into Rebecca's own torchlight. There was sheer terror written all over her face.

'Can you?' whispered Rebecca. 'D'you think you could – ?'

The danger was obvious. The tunnel through there was completely unstable. Little stones and showers of dust were still slithering down on top of Mara: one wrong move in there might bury them both.

'I'll try,' whispered Lucy.

She slithered through the gap easily. Rebecca watched from her own safe vantage point as Lucy inched forward on her elbows until she reached Mara. There were some more light falls of debris. Nothing serious. Rebecca's face and hands were soaked with cold perspiration.

'Careful, Lucy. Careful. Try and clear her face – don't make any sudden movements – '

Delicately, fingers moving lightly, Lucy started to scoop the fallen debris away from Mara's face until the nose and mouth were clear. Then she bent her face close to Mara's and listened.

The waiting was dreadful.

Then there came a moaning sound, just as she'd heard earlier.

'Mara!' cried Rebecca in joy.

Mara's irregular breathing became more even and at last her eyes opened. She stared up at Lucy in astonishment.

'I think Rebecca only just found you in time,' Lucy said solemnly.

Mara was in a dazed state. It was some moments

before she could speak and when she did, she sounded in a wild delirium.

'Weren't you looking for a grotto?' she whispered.

Lucy's eyes widened in surprise. But she quickly put a finger to her lips, like a nurse.

'Sssh. Don't speak. Don't try and move. We've both got to keep very, very still while Rebecca goes and gets help.'

Mara closed her eyes and Rebecca stared through the gap at her anxiously.

But then, after a few moments, she opened her eyes again and gave an indignant little snort.

'What are you looking so dramatic about, anyway?'

Rebecca smiled and shook her head and started to edge her way backwards out of the tunnel – convinced that Mara seemed to be in her right mind, after all.

13
Dismissing the Problems

It took an hour to get Mara out, because the men had to make the tunnel safe first. Lucy Hubbard stayed with her the whole time.

Six vehicles waited by the church while the rescue operation took place. There was an ambulance, a police car, a police van which had brought the special equipment, Papa's big black car, Miss Welbeck's car and Mr Hubbard's small blue saloon. It was still a very dark night, with no moon.

One of the ambulancemen attended to Rebecca's hands and bandaged them and then she was allowed to sit with Tish and the other three in Papa's car. Mr and Mrs Hubbard sat waiting inside the blue saloon car. Mrs Barrington, who'd given permission for the five friends to sit with Papa until Mara was brought safely out, sat with Miss Welbeck.

They brought Mara out on a stretcher. She smiled and waved and everybody got out of their cars and cheered, even Miss Welbeck. Lucy walked behind the stretcher, supported by a police constable, her cape wrapped warmly round her.

They all tried to get close to Mara as she was lifted into the ambulance. Papa took her small hand in his big one and gazed down into her face, long and hard. Then Mara asked for Rebecca to come up into the ambulance.

In silence she put her arms round Rebecca's neck and hugged her.

As Rebecca stepped down from the ambulance, they closed the doors. Then she turned and saw a small man in rimless spectacles. He was wearing a coat over his dark blue pin-striped suit. It was *the* man! Rebecca recognized him at once.

For a moment, her stomach seemed to turn right over.

But he was smiling and reaching his arms out to Lucy.

148

'Daddy!' cried Lucy, embracing him.

The five friends watched in astonishment.

'It was Lucy's father behind the tombstone then!' whispered Elf.

'I don't get it,' said Rebecca.

Mrs Hubbard came over and joined her husband and daughter. She looked very subdued. Miss Welbeck was standing nearby in a white fur coat, thanking one of the police officers but at the same time watching the Hubbard family.

'Trebizon's been a flop for you, hasn't it Lucy?' said Mr Hubbard, an arm round her small shoulders. 'Even your mother realises that. It hasn't worked out for me, either. I've been hopeless without your mother – I even thought of kidnapping you from here, just to get *her* back.'

'K-kidnapping me!' gasped Lucy.

'That's right.' Her father nodded. 'Every time you phoned I could tell how miserable you were. It was bad enough having to play second fiddle to your mother's grand design for you, as though I didn't count! But for you not to be happy here – that was the last straw!'

'But I'm going back to daddy now,' said Mrs Hubbard quickly. 'I'm leaving at half-term. I'll get a teaching job locally. We decided that this evening. And, of course, you'll have to leave when I do. Mrs Barrington's made that quite clear to us.'

'The whole thing's been a disaster,' added Mr Hubbard.

Rebecca & Co. were so fascinated by all this that they just stood there, open-mouthed, quite deliberately

149

eavesdropping. Joan Barrington came over and broke them up.

'Now, you lot, it's late. Papa's waiting to drive you back to Court House. He can take Lucy, too.'

She went and got Lucy.

'Say goodnight to your parents. You can see them in the morning.' Her voice was quite gentle. 'You've been a brave girl – so has Rebecca Mason – and I want you both to have hot baths and some cocoa and a good night's sleep.'

The Hubbards watched the ambulance draw away through Churchgate. A minute later, Papa's car bounced off along the track across the school grounds to Court House, with all the girls on board. Lucy's parents looked sad.

Miss Welbeck came over and spoke to them before getting in her car.

'I'm just taking Joan Barrington back to the boarding house. Could we meet up at my home after that? Perhaps you'd like a hot drink, and really, there's quite a lot to talk about.'

Rebecca and Tish and Sue lay in their beds, still wide awake although it would soon be eleven o'clock. Rebecca had told them the story of how she'd found Mara, reliving every moment.

'Curly was so relieved!' said Tish. She'd phoned him the minute they'd got back to Court House. 'They were turning grey with worry over at Syon. They think you're terrific, Rebeck.'

'So do we,' added Sue.

Finally, as they got very sleepy, their thoughts turned to Lucy.

'Isn't it funny to think *she* was the one who might have got kidnapped!' observed Tish.

'There's another funny thing,' said Rebecca. 'Now she's going I suddenly realise I'm going to miss her.'

'What, in Court House?' asked Sue.

'No. That's been a pain in the neck. In class, I mean. I've quite enjoyed trying to beat her in English and French and not always coming top.'

To Rebecca's surprise, Tish murmured her agreement.

'You're right. She's better at maths than me and it was getting boring coming top. I've got really good at maths, just trying to keep up with her.'

'You two amaze me!' said Sue. Then she giggled. 'I can see I've been missing out. What a pity Lucy doesn't play the violin.'

But as she lay there thinking, Sue began to get bothered about Lucy. Finally, with a huge yawn, she said:

'It's a shame really. She didn't even have a boy friend – it was her father she kept phoning. She can't help the way she is. Maybe we'd have turned out like that, if we'd had Mother Hubbard for a mother.'

On that sobering note, they all went to sleep.

The log fire burned brightly in Miss Welbeck's sitting room. The Irish coffee was delicious, warm and comforting after the cold ordeal of waiting by the church. Mr and Mrs Hubbard began to feel at ease.

Lionel Hubbard, in particular, found it a relief to be able to talk after all the tensions of the past few weeks. Miss Welbeck was not the sort of person he often came across in his job with the insurance firm, but he was beginning to feel a healthy respect for this woman who ran Trebizon. It was curious, the way he could talk to her freely.

'We know Lucy's very clever and we've always wanted the best for her, both of us,' he said. 'But in the last year it's become an absolute obsession with Mary. It's got too much of a good thing. Moving away from home to live in here as a teacher, so we could get the reduction in fees, and she could keep a close eye on Lucy...ridiculous! I didn't count any more. It was breaking our marriage up - '

Mrs Hubbard stared down at the carpet.

'Don't go on, darling. We've agreed it was a mistake. We're both agreed on that now.' She looked up at Miss Welbeck, very unhappily. 'I'm sorry our daughter's turned out to have these behaviour problems. She's a complete misfit here. We quite understand that you must want her to leave.'

'Want her to leave?'

Miss Welbeck leaned forward and warmed her hands in front of the fire.

'I don't want her to leave. I think Lucy will fit in very well, given a little time. As for the fee situation, I'm sure the Governors can look at that kindly. Lucy is an obvious candidate for a closed award.'

Mr and Mrs Hubbard looked at one another in astonishment: and sudden pride.

'But surely – ' began Lionel Hubbard. 'Mrs Barrington says she refuses to have her in Court House any longer – '

'Certainly!' agreed Miss Welbeck. 'She must go into Juniper House with girls of her own age. She'll have to observe all the restrictions they observe. She can continue to have her lessons with Form III Alpha, though. You see, it's perfectly simple. Academically, Lucy is way ahead of her age group and belongs with the older girls. Socially, she's immature. She's actually young for her age. Just a baby! She simply isn't ready to *live* with the middle school girls, but she is ready to take lessons with them. I'm sure the arrangement will work well.'

The Hubbards got up to go. They were still subdued – although delighted. But Mrs Hubbard wasn't a person who could remain subdued for very long. Maternal pride started bubbling up to the surface again.

'We're thrilled that you think Lucy has such promise!' she exclaimed at the front door. She turned to her husband with a look of triumph: 'You see, darling? Miss Welbeck doesn't think Lucy's a misfit. So my idea of bringing her here was right all along. Perhaps we ought to think again about my leaving so soon. Perhaps I should at least stay on until the end of the term – '

As the principal opened the front door, she didn't mince her words.

'You're the real misfit at Trebizon, you know, Mary. The trial arrangement hasn't been a success. I hate to say this, but I would rather you kept firmly to your resolve and resigned at half-term.'

'Of – of course, Miss Welbeck.'

Lionel Hubbard gave the principal of Trebizon an approving nod and gently steered his wife to the car.

As soon as they'd gone, Miss Welbeck went to her study and looked up the private telephone number of George Leonodis in Athens.

It had occurred to her once that Lucy Hubbard and Mara Leonodis were both in the same boat, each of them cursed with an over-protective parent. It looked as though she might have solved Lucy's problem. Now she had to try, yet again, to solve Mara's.

When she got the Greek shipowner on his ex-directory line, she explained that his daughter was in the local hospital. She wasn't seriously hurt, but it might be a good idea for him to fly across and visit her. It would also provide the opportunity for the two of them to meet, as they'd never done so.

They could have a good, long talk together.

Mara spent Sunday in hospital. X-rays showed that no bones were broken, but she was badly cut and bruised in places. Now she needed rest and quiet for at least twenty-four hours, to get over the shock of it all.

However, Rebecca, Tish & Co. were allowed to visit her on the Sunday afternoon and bring Curly with them.

Mara was overjoyed to see them, but she was worried because her father was flying over from Athens in his private 'plane. In fact Papa and Miss Welbeck had just looked in to tell her that they were on their way to the airport at Exonford. The 'plane was expected to land at five o'clock.

'He's coming to take me away from Trebizon,' wailed Mara. 'I know he is.'

They all told her not to be silly. She'd never been in any danger of being kidnapped and Miss Welbeck was most likely going to the airport especially to put in a good word for her.

But they were worried, all the same.

They gave her all the latest school news, just to take her mind off it. How Lucy would be staying, but going into Juniper. How Joss Vining was leaving and what a blow it was for Rebecca – Tish told her that. And how the roast potatoes had been as hard as iron at lunch time because of a power cut.

An hour after her friends had left, Mara's father arrived.

He strode down the ward, gold teeth flashing in his bronzed face, impeccably suited, his arms full of flowers. Nurses scurried forward to take them and put them in water, exclaiming over them, as George Leonodis sat down on the bed and embraced his daughter.

Then he drew away from her, looking at the bruises on her face. There were tears of emotion in his eyes and he spoke in their own language.

'My poor little girl! What a terrible business!'

He took her hand and held it tightly.

'I have something important to say to you,' he said.

Mara's hopes plunged. She closed her eyes, waiting for the words –

'I am sending Papa back to Athens.'

Mara's eyes fluttered open in disbelief.

'Daddy!'

'I've been given a severe talking to by your Miss Welbeck,' smiled Mr Leonodis. 'What a pity we've never met before. A clever, beautiful English woman. As a matter of fact, I am taking her out to dinner tonight. She has promised to show me round the town. It's a very quiet, peaceful sort of place she says.'

'What – what else did she say to you?' asked Mara in wonderment.

'She told me that Papa is much too conspicuous and that his presence here has done nothing but attract attention to you and place you in danger. That you nearly died in that tunnel last night and if you had done so, it would – in this indirect way – have been partly my own fault.'

'Did she really say all that?' exclaimed Mara.

Nobody – but nobody – had ever spoken to her father like that before.

'She did. As a matter of fact, I think she would have liked to give me 5000 lines. She also told me that if I'm really concerned about your safety, the very best thing I can do is see that you're treated in every way as a perfectly ordinary member of the middle school at Trebizon. So you'll merge in with the other girls and be anonymous. She also explained that she has perfectly satisfactory arrangements for looking after the girls who are in her care, without any interference from me, thank you very much!'

'Oh, Daddy!' Mara started to cry, she was so happy.

'Forgive me, Mara.' He embraced her again. 'Forgive me for loving you to the point of stupidity.'

'It was all Linda Grigoris' fault!' wept Mara happily.

'Trust her to go and get herself kidnapped!'

'Remind me of the names of the two girls who saved your life last night,' Mr Leonodis said before he left. 'I'd like to show them my appreciation.'

'Rebecca Mason and Lucy Hubbard.'

'Rebecca – one of your special friends, yes? But I've not heard of this Lucy Hubbard before except that she was the little madwoman who locked you up in the first place.'

'I know just what you can do for Lucy!' said Mara. 'You see, she is rather mad – and something she's mad about is this grotto.'

'Grotto?' The shipowner looked puzzled. 'And Rebecca?'

'Oh, Daddy. I've just thought! I know exactly what you can do for Rebecca!'

Lucy had been right. There was a grotto at Trebizon. The nobleman who'd built the manor house in the eighteenth century had made it in the grounds, near the church, especially for his little daughter, the Ladye Emily. Its main entrance had been through a doorway in a grassy hill and down some steps. But, for whimsy's sake he'd constructed a second secret entrance via the underground tunnel from the church crypt.

Just before the tunnel had caved in on her, Mara had caught a glimpse of it ahead, in her torch beam, an enchanting vision of stone cherubs and underground waterfalls and springs. After Emily's death, the nobleman had commanded both entrances to be blocked up and no-one was allowed to refer again to the existence of the grotto. But Lucy had found a mention of it in the old book she'd bought – and Mara, quite by accident, had located it!

Restoring the grotto became a special Juniper House project for the rest of that term, with Lucy Hubbard as project leader. With the help of funds from Mr Leonodis, they made a fine job of it and Rebecca, Tish and Sue went to see it on the last day of term.

The original entrance in a bank beyond the church, hidden beneath long grass and wild flowers for more than two hundred years, had been opened up and the marble steps down into the grotto now shone as new. A fountain, fed by a freshwater spring, had been repaired and played amongst statues of cherubs and little wild animals, which had all been cleaned up and mended. A waterfall danced down on the far side of the cave and the entrance to the secret tunnel, which had now been blocked up for safety's sake, could just be glimpsed.

'It's simply beautiful,' sighed Rebecca. 'Can't you just imagine the little Ladye Emily spending all those happy, carefree childhood hours here – all that time ago?'

'No wonder her father couldn't bear ever to look at it again, after she died,' said Tish.

'But now it's a memorial to her,' said Sue. 'Our juniors can come and play here, whenever they want, just the way *she* used to. You've got to hand it to Lucy Hubbard. She's got tons of imagination.'

They emerged from the grotto into spring sunshine.

'It's been a marvellous term,' said Rebecca.

They'd all stayed on over half-term for the big concert, which had raised a great deal of money for the Children's

Fund. Both Sue and Chris were proud to have played in the orchestra and to have met backstage the famous stars from all over the world who'd given their services free. It was ample reward for all their hard work, and for missing the fun on the float.

Afterwards the Concert Committee had thrown a party for helpers in the oak-panelled dining hall at Garth College. The girls voted it the best party they'd ever been to.

After half-term, to Sue's delight, Marjorie Spar won the Hilary Camberwell Music Scholarship, narrowly beating Nicola Hodges. Sue liked Marjorie, who as well as being musical – a promising 'cellist – was athletic, too. Just like Sue the year before, she'd had to give up her place in the junior hockey team to concentrate on winning the scholarship.

During the spring term some boy-girl friendships blossomed – like Curly and Mara's – while others withered and died. Virginia Slade finally broke it off with Tish's brother, Robbie, and started going round with a Sixth Form boy at Garth. Tish said that Robbie had taken it very well, considering, and had resolved to study hard for his big summer exams and never to look at a girl again.

'Except he says if it's any help he'll give you some games of tennis next term, Rebeck. Now that Joss won't be here.'

Tennis!

In the last weeks of term, Rebecca played with Joss Vining almost every day and her game improved apace.

'Honestly Rebecca!' Joss said one day. 'If *only* you

could get a sponsor and go in for some competitions these holidays! If you did well – you might be able to convince the County selectors that you're worth promoting.'

'I'm hoping – well, I have got a chance of being sponsored,' Rebecca had replied.

At last the letter arrived. Official confirmation from Leonodis Shipping Lines that they were prepared to sponsor Rebecca Mason in tennis competitions during the Easter holidays, with details of the arrangements. She would be staying with a kind Greek family in London and Papa and a car would be at her disposal!

'Yes, it's been a marvellous term,' Tish agreed. She gave Rebecca her wide smile. 'Maybe next term will be even better.'

'After all,' said Sue, linking arms with the two of them, 'it'll be the tennis term, won't it?'

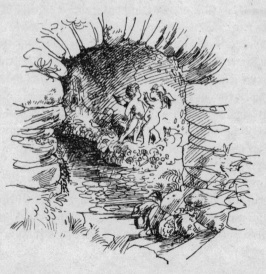